John G. Whittier

SNOW-BOUND

A Winter Idyl

By
JOHN GREENLEAF WHITTIER

WITH PREFACE
BY
HENRY. L. WILLIAMS

NEW YORK
HURST & COMPANY
PUBLISHERS

PREFACE.

John Greenleaf Whittier was born on the seventeenth day of December, 1807. The occurrence was at Haverhill, Mass., on the Merrimac's bank, in what he called "the one dear spot on all the globe." At another time, he saw the Mother State more truly, as "a rough, bleak and hard land." But no other part of our country bears a closer resemblance to what Sir Walter Scott deemed "meet nurse for a poetic child," namely, Caledonia. Here, or not so far distant, were born, contemporaneously, the luminaries of the literary firmament of the 'Forties and 'Fifties. With our subject, they form a constellation not easily cast into the shade by a body in any other part of the United States : Lowell, Longfellow, Holmes, Emerson, Bryant, Hawthorne, and—why not include the satellites, Duganne, Saxe, Street, etc.

Whittier came of that Quaker parentage, ostensibly placid but in heart turbulent, accepting asserted superiority with inward resentment, difficult to rebuff, tenacious wherever they got a hold as climbing ivy. They had many a stubborn conflict with the Puritans, in this region. Hence, a double combativeness marked the young " Friend " as its own, from infancy, and age did not efface the mark. Between school and meeting-house, he could boast that he did " not heed the sceptic or fear the blinded bigot."

His father was a farmer, on that ungrateful ground which the Westerner scoffs at as scarcely sprouting black-eyed beans! The boy spent his youth breaking up this mantle of stones, only interesting to the geologist. But do not think him, like the born pastoral poets, Blomfield, Hogg, and the inspired clods, generally. At least, these had the long wintry evenings for boisterous recreations, which so enliven their pages, after the plodding steps, the sodden furrow, and the sleepy early morning drive to town. On the contrary, winter was the thrifty New Englander's busiest season. His garret became a workshop, where he and his family and, eke, the help, hammered in the pegs of his own whittling, to complete the coarse boots for the negro slaves on the cotton and rice plantations, for whom likewise hummed the Lowell mills and the Concord looms.

The steer-tender and horse-guider became a "shoe-tapper." Where was the counterpart to the picturesque scene of the ambitious youth sprawling before the great wood fire and scrawling or sketching with a charred brand upon the shingle or the grain-shovel back? The little cobbler pegged together scores of pairs of brogans for the Southern field hand, and went shoeless half the year; he apostrophizes "the Little Barefoot Boy" as "a prince," but to be a republican when grown up—hating and striving to overthrow the set frame that made child labor a virtue!

The sole relief in the workshop, as in the field, was in the current tattle;—the young toilers exchanged stories, varying in tone, and the elders related grim legends of the days when there were wild Indians. The incipient poet was to repeat them with adornment and enhancement as you will see in his " Legends," one day. He saved much out of the enchanting past when the unromantic Puritan would willingly have had it all die with the last sumach plume. Then he relished, the grave lad, the local events —such as " the Line Fence " squabbles— with racy, jesty humor, useful advice against the rustic bane of " lawing," and given by the author a moral of humanity and brotherly love—quite after the Penn manner.

Sitting on the line fences or the vast stone ones, bristling with woodchucks, snakes and brambles, who should hap along but that good genius of the boy unappreciated—" the Ugly Duckling "—but the sprite that always meets Fortunatus in his plight. It was a tramp—the Bohemian, who roves, since Homer, or Villon if you prefer a nigh cry—

a vagabond "spouter," as the word went
then. A rarity, for the English beadle,
become the New England constable, made
the wayward-farer's saunter a burden. It
was, too, a Scot—a Scottish idler! unique
when the best settlers in the new States were
the expelled crofters and victims of the Suth-
erland Clearances, to make deer- or sheep-
runs. An Irish or a negro wanderer might
be seen, but a Gael was novel under any
aspect. The jovial, loquacious Gaberlunzie
Man enchanted the green boy. In his own
dialect, Whittier writes him down as " a
pawky auld carle," and a *canny* one, since he
obtained a good meal and a doze in the barn
for a mouthful of ranting. But among the
hotch-pot scraps were lines of Robert Burns.
The two plowboys poetic, met on the level.
Whittier understood that men should stop

and lament over a daisy cut in twain by the coulter, though the ocean separated them.

The wandering *callant* had filled his little friend with the longing to hold the whole posy of which he had tendered a few slips. Whittier was not content until his schoolmaster, informing him that Burns' works were collected, presented him with such a nosegay off Helicon hills. What Plutarch is to Cæsars, Euclid to Laplaces, Blackstone to Lincolns, and Shakespeare to Dumases, Burns was for the truly American poet. The untaught peasant saved this peasant from "the tyranny of the Greeks and the Romans"! Whittier had shown how easily one may write genuine poetry and not be "classical"!

Whittier babbled at once in numbers, "but the numbers came." With them was the

savor of forbidden sweets. Imagine the
consternation—akin to that in the Quaker
household when little Benjamin was dis-
covered painting the child's portrait with
Indian ochres and the brush made of the
cat's tail! A Quaker poet! hymns—pass-
able!—but doggerel, whimsicalities, even pa-
triotic verse urging war for freedom! But
you no more remove a poet's proclivity by
argument than a broadbrim, even before the
King. The pent-up outflow was coming,
and while it flowed in the first mold—the
Burns'—the clearness, sparkle, vitality, an
irresistible gladful gush convinced good and
sober judges, stirred into justness not leni-
ence, that much might be expected from the
ripe fruit, if this were but the *Green Leaf*.

He used idiomatic Saxon, such as Cobbett,
the English grammarian, recently inculcated.

Ere long, he laid aside the distortions of old
French and Gaelic which compose Lowland
jargon, and retained of the fervid, caustic
Burns model only the leading traits, common
to all poets, being patriots, truth-seekers,
lovers of the beautiful, discerners of delicate
cates. Mr. Coffin, the schoolmaster, had
better have corrected the terrible American
tendency to recklessness, by which the purist
in poesy is wantonly shocked. Without
bending wholly to the " tyranny of corre-
sponding sound," Draconian mark of perfection ! how condone in a Whittier—a
pedagogue, at one time—" saw " and " for "
coupled as consonant, or the final syllable of
" orchestra " to rhyme with " play " ? And
they are not solitary blotches.

So far good as to the embryo songster ;
but while vociferating verse is well, putting it

in print for public examination is proper and pleasanter to a writer who now had no reason to fear. Happily, it is a poor and unrepresentative Massachusetts village without the school blackboard, the pulpit sounding-board and the printing-press. In fact, Haverhill had a gazette! Of this, anon. But this was too near the source of origin, the sort of mock-guiltiness—shamefacedness, at all events, attending publication by a beginner, surrounded Whittier's maiden effort. "The Deist," which was the title, formidable and forbidding anywhere but in sanctimonious New England, was taken a little way off. The Nazarenes might not have recognized their own "prodigy child." The editor was astonished at the youth of the author; he had the glowing lines set defiantly in type. The first impression was carried to the village, and the author's sister, the trusted intermediary, transported it forthwith out to her brother, working in the potato patch. Baron Buffon, who could not write unless he put on lace cuffs in his sumptuous study, certainly would not acknowledge this too bucolic a Virgil among the rows of " Early Rose " as a brother clerk. Leaning on his hoe, Whittier read his virginal product, as Burns might his diatribes to the thistles. After the flush of gladness—the chill of modesty of the plowboy rhyming—and daintily—for poaching on the manor of the collegiate-drilled ! He was awed at being hailed as a *scald* among those neighbors, who esteemed the literary as witless or wizards. But the poet's sister was more proud than he, and more desirous of the sheen to gild the house. She not merely drew away the veil with which the timid lyrist strove to drape himself, but ran to the editor of the piece, and conducted him to behold the wonder of Haverhill.

The editor caught his protégé still in the potato-patch! Decidedly, after this, King Louis XV was not so wrong as to wear the *solanum* bloom in his buttonhole—Whittier has proven that romance may blossom among the useful tubers as fragrantly as among the exuberant tuberoses.

Fortunately, the editor of acumen was above the earth: it was the heroic and undaunted Apostle of Emanicipation—William Lloyd Garrison. He was to be the *Garrison* of that fort whose thunders shook down the ancient and redoubtable temple castle of the slaveholding Philistines: The Arch-Abolitionist. On questioning the **blushing lad, he quickly concluded that**

nature had been bounteous ; 'twas the curb,
not the spur, was needed. He recom-
mended schooling. In the interim, the
local seminary would suffice.

Fate continued propitious : the student's
boarding-house was kept by a gentleman
whose leisure from carving and drawing up
scores, was given to the Muses—at least, he
edited the weekly *Gazette*. Its " Lion's
mouth " yawned for the talented boarder's
productions. But the academic instruction
was costly and, still among the Puritans, the
" Vanity Fair " was unknown for literary
wares. The pupil turned school-teacher to
earn the fees to carry him over the next
term. It was pouring out of the spigot
what went in at the bunghole. Whittier
was studying the divine Jeremy Taylor, to
profit ; among the wise dicta of that coun-

sellor, one perceived : " That friend is the
best chosen, by whom one can best recover
comfort and assistance." Such a friend was
in that dear, true Lloyd Garrison. He was
in Boston, where he remembered " the Marvellous Boy," whom he did not intend should
perish in his prime in a potato bed. He
prevailed on the proprietor of the *American
Manufacturer*, an original trades-organ,
invented before our time—to make the
young tyro its weekly contributor. The
stipend of nine dollars came as a staff
rather than a crutch to the struggler,
divided between farm and office. But this
was a time-saver : again, the alternative was
offered—to renounce the endeared pen or
let the homestead go to the dogs ! He
clung to the sill, and in uncongenial travail,
waited till 1830.

How galling was that abject, penurious, niggling business to an ethereal nature! Around him the ideal was a waterhead to turn mill wheels; the wheels to race shuttles and spindles; the furious machines to set the pace for haggard men, women and children; a few lucky-unlucky men were allowed to torture the sterile ground to grow food for the caged human squirrels. The mill waste poisoned the fishes and summer flies; the smoke banished the birds and obscured the sun. All resembled the English Black Country. The inventor in request was for machinery, not phantasms of the brain. Design lace bonnet epics; paint muslin, not pictures.

Whittier "kicked at the pricks"; he irked at the contrasts of the mill-plutocrat's daughter lolling on her piano-stool and

thrumming operatic *arias*, while the " Blind
Hannahs" moaned sad ballads in binding
shoes for a pittance. The fire and energy
of the ancient denunciators of injustice
burst forth over the renewal of Old World
despotism and inhumanity in the New One.
He threw comfort to the white slave, and
exposed to the unheeding public "the Pris-
oner for Debt." Withering, thrilling, he
tugged at the bonds, relics of the Dark
Ages. Everybody felt the incongruity of
the Independence Day joy-bells flinging
their derisive clang r into the cell, where
languished the Revolutionary veteran for a
paltry due, overweighted by the legal costs.

"Down with the law that binds man
thus !"

It was Howard, or Fry, become Tyrtæus!
Periodicals such as the *Yankee*, the N. E.

Weekly Review, etc., of insignificant circula-
tion but, mark! extensively copied through-
out the settled Union and by the cheap
miscellanies of England, carried Whittier's
name afar; his "Minstrel Girl" might
march with Moore's "Minstrel Boy,"
and his "*fugitive* verse" received welcome
in cot and cabin, if not yet in the drawing-
room. But such bay leaves were as those
coins in the Arabian Tales, magically
changed to worthlessness in the chest. The
American Burns had to go back to the
corn-hoeing, again, when a second call to-
wards his destined course was gladly heard.

Once more, a good man proved the best
friend. His pieces, wedding beauty and
sentiment with rectitude of conduct, in the
Review, appeased the keen criticism while
exciting the amity of the Editor. It was

George D. Prentice, summoned to Louis-
ville to make himself and the *Journal* fa-
mous and valuable as a civilizer in the South-
west. Like Garrison previously, he insisted
to the proprietor of the organ he quitted,
that the man for the post was " the young
rhymer up the country." The invitation
found the Farmer-versifer, as was his wont,
out mending fences and at other farm work.
He was still weary of it, and embraced the
harbinger with rapture, saying with his frank-
ness so juvenile :

" I could not have been more surprised
had I been offered the Crown of England ! "

Hastening to the desk, he took up the
Review, and it is high eulogy to say that,
after the brilliant Prentice, Whittier main-
tained it a readable paper. The year 1830
was therefore pleasant and gratifying—the

welkin was harmonious and instructive. His creative energy might freely expand, his ideas were commended, his projects acclaimed, his drafts admiringly criticized. His associates were Yale collegians, for the seat of the *Review* was Hartford,—afterwards to be professors, pundits, authorities, oracles, but, in after-life, they were not so elevated as not to confer with him on intellectual progress.

Incredible! the reek of the glebe still again drew him back to the homestead: his father's death placed him master of the repeated dilemma, between soil and study. Samson, to choose between the free life when he could send firebrand-carrying foxes into the enemy's ranks, or bend to the beam of the flour mill. His plaint at the quandary is exhaled by the future judge in "Maud

Muller," wondering if, with Maud by his side, the pastoral life on the old farm would not be happier than one on the bench.

In his rustication the Sage of Haverhill consoled himself by collecting his strays! it was his first folding of the local legends in prose and verse. He hoped that he could resume that tantalizing life of slippered ease among the learned, when storm clouds were rising and the reader's lamp was useless unless turned into a beacon of war. In the Abolition of Slavery in the South a movement came down out of the Utopian air, and assumed portentous form like the released bottled-up Oriental genie. The darkness was the precursor of the Civil War.

It was the armed attack, no longer the theoretical and rhetorical one, born with the Revolution. The previous call had been meekly for the removal, not the destruction, of the Institution. The manumission of the British West Indian slaves had been done by purchase; of the French West Indians, by the great Revolution, coherently; and in the Spanish American Possessions, the bondage was rotting away. All were tokens that the *plant* was doomed, and, indeed, ceased to be profitable unless the slaveholders also controlled the government exchequer. It was linked with the tariff, this domestic thraldom. In the North, the cold aided the foreign laborers to kill it; in the West, its upward surge was strenuously resisted. Poetically, none had a word for its retention; indeed, the cry for its destruction prevailed in all rhymes that matched " grave " and " slave," and " free " and " agree." The state of the

South blurred with the popular phrases of
" Free   Trade."   " Free   Seas," " Free
Speech."

Schemes of imitating England and buy-
ing off the trammels, rose north and south.

But this smote severely the masses, who
neither owned slaves nor the supplying
marts for their wants. It was obvious that
as soon as no longer driven to work for
others, the black—only too human—would
work solely for his daily needs, where the
climate exacted no storing up for rainy days.
Hence, with purchased freedom, the liber-
ators, under the new and mountainous tax
of redemption, would have no more sugar,
rice, tobacco, rum, cotton ! All the stills,
mills, factories, north, would stand idle;
and alike the planter, on his veranda, and
the millionaire manufacturer, in his parlor,

would pine and peak as their idle capital waned.

This resource impossible, the extremists declared war upon the slaveholder simply as a slaveholder, like a Cain with his doom on his brow. They said—not merely in safety on watchtowers in the North, but on the border and even within "Slaveria," that they would break the yoke and unbind the burden.

By race and creed, Whittier was matured for this propaganda. Bred and born as a bard to it, he readily resorted to prophetical invocations and invectives. The Anti-Slavery cause lacked a mouthpiece, here it was, eagerly thrust forth, yet to blow down Jericho.

The society made him secretary—Druid, oracle, horn-blower in the Scriptural sense, and his breath was from the sacred cave. He began the cult in his native place, and he did not leave this burning plowshare half-way in the furrow. In 1833, a long article—one of those fiery shafts thrown into the hostile ranks to denote relentless warfare—" the Curse of Slavery," you see the plain-dealer does not haggle with words! appeared in the *Journal*, of " Little Rhody " —a bulwark of opposition to tyranny. At the same time, as a javelin, like a weaver's beam, he thrust with his " Voices of Freedom." The poet's chord of Self passed now out of sight, and the Struggling Cause of Humanity Unchained—the greater Prometheus with unveiled light,—recognized with rapture a forcible recruit with a noble simplicity equaling his ardor. But he was at once hailed as the ensign.

Whittier gave up the farm at last, thoroughly worn out, and edited that local *Gazette* in which his immature lispings had been ventilated, and which he diverted into the Abolition organ. In the heart of the State devoted to making goods for the slave-holders—it was a testimonial to his personal powers that his fellow-citizens elected him representative to the State House, to promulgate his ultra and subversive views. As poet of liberation, he could hope no patrons among the Mill-ocrats ; as a rabid politician, he was ruled out of the pale. The opposition remained as wet tow to the torch ; time came when the agitator was repulsed ; he was ostracized. Like his progenitors for the belief in freedom, he was banished. In 1837, he was harbored in New York.

That cosmopolitan city, the Geneva of

America, welcomed all political exiles though
" mobbing" them a little, by the way ; the
Anti-Slavery Society had quarters here and
the homeless bard was the secretary; this
bird was growing under persecution, no
longer a bearer of the olive branch but a
raven, with cypress and hyssop ; croaking of
the Impending Crisis.

The Quaker clarion was enlisted for a war.
Meanwhile, he was wise to flee Boston which
expelled the other saints in Garrison, Phil-
lips, and their over-fervid brethren. The
Yankees had conquered everything, said
Webster, " but their prejudices." The
makers of plantation brogues could not
stomach the would-be free emancipators of
their best customers. " The Black Abolitionist Laureate " ate the bitter bread of
exile. All fraternal ties snapped in the fiery

furnace of partisan strife. The radical Red
Cap of Liberty ill accorded with the Drab-
coat and Broad-brim. In the City of Penn
and Franklin, where Whittier conducted the
Freeman, the mob rose upon him, sacked the
office and threatened to make bullets for his
black Abolitionist heart of the types in which
some of his finest exhortations were set.
Nevertheless, he urged bloodless measures ;
he recognized that slavery was constituted
legally ; his opposition was to the extension
of the evil. Counter to such comrades as
Garrison, he counselled gradual and peaceful
emancipation. The Southern sympathizers
sneeringly responded to this compromise
that he could look calmly on torture, then,
who would not look on war.

To recuperate after this contest with ac-
tual arms with the mob, Whittier retired to

Amesbury, Mass., hereafter his home, if the agitator could be said to have a home. It was 1840.

During the Mexican War, the Anti-Slavery ram was laid by ; it was not rusting, but being tempered for the coming combat by persecution, reviling, stripes, jail, law of the regular bench and Mr. Justice Lynch. The philanthropist vein shows in the sequestered poet in his " Angels of Buena Vista," where he foresees the ministering spirits of the Christian Commission on *our* Buena Vistas. The example of mercy and charity he firmly evinces cannot be "wholly lost in this evil world of ours." The optimist distinguishes himself from the despairing Byrons and Poes.

The annexation of Texas was a reinforcement to the Slave States. Consequently the

Abolitionists revived their attacks. Whittier sprang to the battle-front. In Washington he bravely edited the *National Intelligencer*, that standard of the Anti-Slavery party (in which appeared " Uncle Tom's Cabin," the volume to crush the South like the Swamp Angel's colossal charge). Under the poet's hand, this became what the *Liberator* was in Boston, a mighty engine to divorce with steel the Caliban that plagued Miranda on the Isle of Beauty. His effusions were outbursts—the shower of vitriol, and not the rose-water of ordinary poets. The discharge swept away the " Northern men with Southern principles," the double-dealing Copper-heads, and tried to rally Unionism.

Confident in the faith of his doctrines when, at last, "the standards of the peoples

plunged together into the thunder-storms,"
of 1860–'5, Whittier acted politically with
the humanitarian school of Lincoln, Greeley
and Garrison, heart and soul. He loudly
said : "I am proud of the part I played in
the Controversy."

But at the old home, he was shouted,
jeered at, hated for injuring trade—it was his
pen that had been poked impertinently in
and hindered the wheels going around. The
perpetual antagonism of those who see in
Pegasus just a horse wasted if not drawing
a load or tracing the furrow. But the un-
prepossessed young were candid ; they rev-
elled on his poetry ; incipient orators tore his
passions to rags ; Billy Lackadays murmured
his " Telling the Bees " ; sea-boys chanted
about the cruel skipper ; and sentimental
misses invaded the book-stores to glean

something new from Whittier. He had found out by nature, not by research, how to make the songs of the people:

> " Give to the dreams of youth,
> With the form of Art, which is beauty,
> The soul of Art, which is Truth."

Strange in an inlander, but having the Briton's love of the ocean, he wrote of it with befitting grandeur, fluency, grave melody and its own incessant caressing to hide the voracity. He sympathized with the fisher and the coaster-folk, and their droll phrases echo in his copies without superfluity of harsh dialect. He rises to the universal concord in the "Three Bells." Here, the English mariner keeps his ship close to the foundering American, through the perilous night, shouting with unflagging voice that he is standing by forever! The

English glory in this ballad ; and, in a
competition in their press about the poet's
standing, it was Whittier's name " that led
all the rest."

But among the laurels, not a bank-note!
Alas ! as we have shown, the lover and
panegyrist of truth, equality, freedom, made
no friends among the enriched who
bought foreign masterpieces for their gal-
leries. Woe ! no munificent Mæcenas for
the Whittiers who reaped the barren honors
of the *Waverley* or the village poets' corner !
The dilettante of Boston set the mode, and
for a crust Poe, Payne, and the innumerable
Chattertons died houseless, cheerless, uncom-
forted, from the Aroostook to the Apalach-
icola.

Whittier's verse starred the omnipresent
press, but the returns were *nil*.   Alone, our

poet's " white blackbird," his " Snow-
Bound," met a publisher who paid a twenty-
five cent royalty.   Another nugget—there
are no more—an advertising editor exchanged
his check for a thousand dollars for a hundred lines.   Of the Civil War, " Barbara
Frietchie " remains the rare memorial that dis-
concerts no one all over the Republic.   True
or false, the fact is no more material than if
Troy once existed, " Stonewall " Jackson's
remorse and respect for " Old Glory " does
him as much honor as the old patriot's fear-
less protection to the banner.   And it is
a dramatic episode, not to be awaited from
a rural poet !

The belligerent Abolitionist disappeared
under the Quaker, when the War ended :
like Sumner and all, he wished to obliterate
all record of the " little difficulty," as native

good-humor soon distinguished it; he desired to "bury in the waters of oblivion all the bitter things I said in the strife." Bitter, that he said? he who sanctified the poet's holy mission? He who promulgated the truth that the child of a common country can be neither a victor nor a defeated foe.

When the Centennial celebration came, it was he as living monument of liberation and enlightenment, and preacher of the faith that "the world was growing better, sweeter and tenderer, with more love in it!" It was Whittier and none other who was pointed out by all hands and unanimously chosen to commemorate verbally the jubilee. His strain was to the date, our young, aspiring, far-reaching, audacious inspiration, without apathy, disbelief, decay, mistrust. Such a contemporary document, therefore, inevitably

concludes with the blast of chanticleer Hope,
always hailing a morning :

"Let the new cycle shame the old !"

Ever after in our boundless country,
Whittier was named "softly as *the* household name," our citizens of foreign origin
sent the poems they learnt the best English
by, to all the remote climes ; widely was he
thus known and endeared.   Translations were
rife, and the lowly worshipped him as they
do Burns, Andersen, Grimm, Jasmin,
Mackay, Dibdin.   As a proof that the
foreigner knew him by heart, on an American woman offering versions of several of
our author's poems in French, they were
immediately detected in the press—from the
familiarity with their impressive ideas in their
former dress.   It was clear that he was another friend of the friendless, consoler of the

discomforted, and enlivener of the young
man—decider at the point of holding fast by
the intellect and its evanescent gains or striving to get the home, barn and acre which he
spurned, for the meed of popularity, reverence and immortality. They found that
Whittier refreshes you when run down,
smoothed where the business cares rasp, spurs
against the check, and sympathizes like the
Royal Psalmist on all occasions. It has been
said of his works that if there were but one
choice in a burning library for a solace after
the disaster, it would be Whittier best to save.
Oh, the stainless page—nothing obscure, for
that obscurity is not necessary if you would
be understood—all the persuasion of the
Beatitudes, and " no vileness in all his life to
no manner of men," Chaucer's perfect knight,
loved by everybody, for he loved all.

Passing the allotted fourscore, Whittier
was to terminate vicissitudes—for, like
Byron, he had realized that "a man should
do something more than write verse!"
in calmness, "regular as infants' breaths."

He walked about in the busy vale, where
"the mill or two" on the Merrimac had
multiplied in a century to ten—the million
spindles being a twentieth part of all in the
United States. The hum of the vast indus-
try lulled him and did not perturb. He
had compensation, for "nature always gives
us more than she takes away." For his
kind wise words, the townsfolk could not
too much honor and venerate him. In
every house was a chair and a corner.
Things had taken a turn from when fathers
rejoiced at a gifted son turning from poetry
—for "poets were always poor," and re-

turned to work ! The rich invited acquaint-
ances to show " the Foremost Puritan Poet
of America." The foreigners—alas ! three
parts of Lowell's population are aliens !
hailed him as a herald of freedom and free
labor ; ameliorators, as the disseminator of
Reforms ; negroes, as their manumittor ;
Quakers, as a worthy Friend ; all men as a
brother.

What literature ! chanting which men
trod the gory battle-ways, and which can be
read to a child—

" Its smiles might play upon an angelic face ;
    Its tears would not stain an angel's cheek."

The lute was meet for the music, the
figure was erect ; not needing the aged pilgrim's staff; in the desert, he had struck
the springs ; if the head bent, so hangs the
matured grain, or the student's and the

thoughtful farmer's; the white side and chin beard enframed ever-energetic features; the deep-set eyes beamed kindly beneath the shielding brows, which had frowned only on wrongs; the forehead was the sage's—generously high and broad. The mouth was more firm than smiling—he had lavished his smiles in his verse!

He read less than he listened to; he wrote little, but he scribbled incessantly on odd pieces of paper as in his youth when paper was scarce; crossing and re-crossing; harmless satires upon themes, events, the neighbors, who prized these playful mentions. He carried on his correspondence until forced to employ the proud young worshippers as amanuenses. He strolled, and sat at the desk, seeing visions not for the prosaic, in the mirror of the inkdish

cup ; reflecting, with his pen gripped ready
for action—

> " Beside the silent sea,
>   I wait the muffled oar ;
> No harm from Him can come to me
>   On ocean or on shore ! "

(It is a picture in exquisite equipoise with
Tennyson's sitting with the open Shake-
speare on his knee, also, waiting for the
Pilot !)

On the morning of the seventh day of
September, 1892, Whittier joined the wel-
coming assembly of kindred spirits on the
farther shore.   He was passing the summer
at a New Hampshire resort.   His remains
were treasured at Amesbury, under the flags
(at half-mast) for which he wrote undying
legends, and while the bells knelled the
eighty-and-four tokens of his age.   In

the Friends' Cemetery, amid all his family,
the acre of rest is the site of the poet and
the patriot lovers' pilgrimage.

As his works were for the race's better-
ment, they remain unfading—never be-
littled, ever-green. Whittier owed nothing to
the so-called New England School—apish
of British precedents; and while thoroughly
American, he is to all men something of
good cheer and to most reading men—all!

Two decades pass, and his place is not
taken.   His works go on and lead upward,
while

> " Th' eternal step of progress beats
>   To the great anthem, calm and slow,
>   Which God repeats."

HENRY L. WILLIAMS.

May, 1907.

SNOW-BOUND.

SNOW-BOUND.

THE sun that brief December day
Rose cheerless over hills of gray,
And, darkly circled, gave at noon
A sadder light than waning moon.
Slow tracing down the thickening sky
Its mute and ominous prophecy,
A portent seeming less than threat,
It sank from sight before it set.
A chill no coat, however stout,
Of homespun stuff could quite shut out,
A hard, dull bitterness of cold,
 That checked, mid-vein, the circling race
 Of life-blood in the sharpened face,
The coming of the snow-storm told.

The wind blew east: we heard the roar
Of Ocean on its wintry shore,
And felt the strong pulse throbbing there
Beat with low rhythm our inland air.

Meanwhile we did our nightly chores,—
Brought in the wood from out of doors,
Littered the stalls, and from the mows
Raked down the herd's grass for the cows;
Heard the horse whinnying for his corn;
And, sharply clashing horn on horn,
Impatient down the stanchion rows
The cattle shake their walnut bows;
While, peering from his early perch
Upon the scaffold's pole of birch,
The cock his crested helmet bent
And down his querulous challenge sent.

Unwarmed by any sunset light
The gray day darkened into night,

A night made hoary with the swarm
And whirl-dance of the blinding storm,
As zigzag wavering to and fro
Crossed and recrossed the wingéd snow:
And ere the early bed-time came
The white drift piled the window-frame,
And through the glass the clothes-line posts
Looked in like tall and sheeted ghosts.

So all night long the storm roared on:
The morning broke without a sun;
In tiny spherule traced with lines
Of Nature's geometric signs,
In starry flake, and pellicle,
All day the hoary meteor fell;
And, when the second morning shone,
We looked upon a world unknown,
On nothing we could call our own.
Around the glistening wonder bent

The blue walls of the firmament,
No cloud above, no earth below,—
A universe of sky and snow !
The old familiar sights of ours
Took marvellous shapes ; strange domes
    and towers
Rose up where sty or corn-crib stood,
Or garden wall, or belt of wood ;
A smooth white mound the brush-pile showed
A fenceless drift what once was road ;
The bridle-post an old man sat
With loose-flung coat and high cocked hat ;
The well-curb had a Chinese roof ;
And even the long sweep, high aloof,
In its slant splendor, seemed to tell
Of Pisa's leaning miracle.

A prompt, decisive man, no breath
Our father wasted : " Boys, a path ! "

Well pleased, (for when did farmer boy
Count such a summons less than joy?)
Our buskins on our feet we drew;
    With mittened hands, and caps drawn low,
    To guard our necks and ears from snow,
We cut the solid whiteness through.
And, where the drift was deepest, made
A tunnel walled and overlaid
With dazzling crystal: we had read
Of rare Aladdin's wondrous cave,
And to our own his name we gave,
With many a wish the luck were ours
To test his lamp's supernal powers.
We reached the barn with merry din,
And roused the prisoned brutes within.
The old horse thrust his long head out,
And grave with wonder gazed about;
The cock his lusty greeting said,
And forth his speckled harem led;

The oxen lashed their tails, and hooked,
And mild reproach of hunger looked;
The hornéd patriarch of the sheep,
Like Egypt's Amun roused from sleep,
Shook his sage head with gesture mute,
And emphasized with stamp of foot.

All day the gusty north-wind bore
The loosening drift its breath before;
Low circling round its southern zone,
The sun through dazzling snow-mist shone.
No church-bell lent its Christian tone
To the savage air, no social smoke
Curled over woods of snow-hung oak.
A solitude made more intense
By dreary voicéd elements,
The shrieking of the mindless wind,
The moaning tree-boughs swaying blind,
And on the glass the unmeaning beat

Of ghostly finger-tips of sleet.

Beyond the circle of our hearth

No welcome sound of toil or mirth

Unbound the spell, and testified

Of human life and thought outside.

We minded that the sharpest ear

The buried brooklet could not hear,

The music of whose liquid lip

Had been to us companionship,

And, in our lonely life, had grown

To have an almost human tone.

As night drew on, and, from the crest

Of wooded knolls that ridged the west,

The sun, a snow-blown traveller, sank

From sight beneath the smothering bank,

We piled, with care, our nightly stack

Of wood against the chimney-back,—

The oaken log, green, huge, and thick,

And on its top the stout back-stick;

The knotty forestick laid apa.t,
And filled between with curious art
The ragged brush ; then, hovering near,
We watched the first red blaze appear,
Heard the sharp crackle, caught the gleam
On whitewashed wall and sagging beam,
Until the old, rude-furnished room
Burst, flower-like, into rosy bloom ;
While radiant with a mimic flame
Outside the sparkling drift became,
And through the bare-boughed lilac-tree
Our own warm hearth seemed blazing free.
The crane and pendent trammels showed,
The Turks' heads on the andirons glowed ;
While childish fancy, prompt to tell
The meaning of the miracle,
Whispered the old rhyme : " *Under the tree*,
When fire outdoors burns merrily,
There the witches are making tea."

The moon above the eastern wood
Shone at its full ; the hill-range stood
Transfigured in the silver flood,
Its blown snows flashing cold and keen,
Dead white, save where some sharp ravine
Took shadow, or the sombre green
Of hemlocks turned to pitchy black
Against the whiteness at their back.
For such a world and such a night
Most fitting that unwarming light,
Which only seemed where'er it fell
To make the coldness visible.

Shut in from all the world without,
We sat the clean-winged hearth about.
Content to let the north-wind roar
In baffled rage at pane and door,
While the red logs before us beat
The frost-line back with tropic heat ;

And ever, when the louder blast
Shook beam and rafter as it passed,
The merrier up its roaring draught
The great throat of the chimney laughed,
The house-dog on his paws outspread
Laid to the fire his drowsy head,
The cat's dark silhouette on the wall
A couchant tiger's seemed to fall;
And, for the winter fireside meet,
Between the andirons' straddling feet,
The mug of cider simmered slow,
The apples sputtered in a row,
And, close at hand the basket stood
With nuts from brown October's wood.

What matter how the night behaved?
What matter how the north-wind raved?
Blow high, blow low, not all its snow
Could quench our hearth-fire's ruddy glow.

O Time and Change !—with hair as gray
As was my sire's that winter day,
How strange it seems, with so much gone
Of life and love, to still live on !
Ah, brother ! only I and thou
Are left of all that circle now,—
The dear home faces whereupon
That fitful firelight paled and shone.
Henceforward, listen as we will,
The voices of that hearth are still ;
Look where we may, the wide earth o'er,
Those lighted faces smile no more.
We tread the paths their feet have worn,
    We sit beneath their orchard-trees,
    We hear, like them, the hum of bees
And rustle of the bladed corn ;
We turn the pages that they read,
    Their written words we 'inger o'er,
But in the sun they cast no shade,

No voice is heard, no sign is made,
    No step is on the conscious floor !
Yet Love will dream, and Faith will trust,
(Since He who knows our need is just,)
Tnat somehow, somewhere, meet we must
Alas for him who never sees
The stars shine through his cypress-trees !
Who, hopeless, lays his dead away,
Nor looks to see the breaking day
Across the mournful marbles play !
Who hath not learned, in hours of faith,
    The truth to flesh and sense unknown,
That Life is ever Lord of Death,
    And love can never lose its own !

We sped the time with stories old,
Wrought puzzles out, and riddles told,
Or stammered from our school-book lore
" The chief of Gambia's golden shore."

How often since, when all the land
Was clay in Slavery's shaping hand,
As if a trumpet called, I've heard
Dame Mercy Warren's rousing word :
" *Does not the voice of reason cry,*
  Claim the first right which Nature gave,
From the red scourge of bondage fly,
  Nor deign to live a burdened slave ! "
Our father rode again his ride
On Memphremagog's wooded side ;
Sat down again to moose and samp
In trapper's hut and Indian camp ;
Lived o'er the old idyllic ease
Beneath St. François' hemlock-trees ;
Again for him the moonlight shone
On Norman cap and bodiced zone ;
Again he heard the violin play
Which led the village dance away,
And mingled in its merry whirl

The grandame and the laughing girl.
Or, nearer home, our steps he led
Where Salisbury's level marshes spread.
    Mile-wide as flies the laden bee ;
Where merry mowers, hale and strong,
Swept, scythe on scythe, their swaths along
    The low green prairies of the sea.
We shared the fishing off Boar's Head,
    And round the rocky Isles of Shoals
    The hake-broil on the drift-wood coals ;
The chowder on the sand-beach made,
Dipped by the hungry, steaming hot,
With spoons of clam-shell from the pot.
We heard the tales of witchcraft old,
And dream and sign and marvel told
To sleepy listeners as they lay
Stretched idly on the salted hay,
Adrift along the winding shores,
When favoring breezes deigned to blow

The square sail of the gundalow
And idle lay the useless oars.
Our mother, while she turned her wheel
Or run the new-knit stocking-heel,
Told how the Indian hordes came down
At midnight on Cochecho town,
And how her own great-uncle bore
His cruel scalp-mark to fourscore.
Recalling, in her fitting phrase,
  So rich and picturesque and free,
  (The common unrhymed poetry
Of simple life and country ways,)
The story of her early days,—
She made us welcome to her home ;
Old hearths grew wide to give us room ;
We stole with her a frightened look
At the gray wizard's conjuring-book,
The fame whereof went far and wide
Through all the simple country side ;

We heard the hawks at twilight play,
The boat-horn on Piscataqua,
The loon's weird laughter far away ;
We fished her little trout-brook, knew
What flowers in wood and meadow grew,
What sunny hillsides autumn-brown
She climbed to shake the ripe nuts down,
Saw where in sheltered cove and bay
The ducks' black squadron anchored lay,
And heard the wild-geese calling loud
Beneath the gray November cloud.

Then, haply, with a look more grave,
And soberer tone, some tale she gave
From painful Sewell's ancient tome,
Beloved in every Quaker home,
Of faith fire-winged by martyrdom,
Or Chalkley's Journal, old and quaint,—
Gentlest of skippers, rare sea-saint !—

Who when the dreary calms prevailed,
And water-butt and bread-cask failed,
And cruel, hungry eyes pursued
His portly presence mad for food,
With dark hints muttered under breath
Of casting lots for life or death,
Offered, if Heaven withheld supplies,
To be himself the sacrifice.
Then, suddenly, as if to save
The good man from his living grave,
A ripple on the water grew,
A school of porpoise flashed in view.
" Take, eat," he said, " and be content ;
These fishes in my stead are sent
By Him who gave the tangled ram
To spare the child of Abraham."
Our uncle, innocent of books,
Was rich in lore of fields and brooks,
The ancient teachers never dumb

Of Nature's unhoused lyceum.

In moons and tides and weather wise,

He read the clouds as prophecies,

And foul or fair could well divine,

By many an occult hint and sign,

Holding the cunning-warded keys

To all the woodcraft mysteries;

Himself to Nature's heart so near

That all her voices in his ear

Of beast or bird had meanings clear,

Like Apollonius of old,

Who knew the tales the sparrows told,

Or Hermes, who interpreted

What the sage cranes of Nilus said;

A simple, guileless, childlike man,

Content to live where life began;

Strong only on his native grounds,

The little world of sights and sounds

Whose girdle was the parish bounds,

Whereof his fondly partial pride
The common features magnified,
As Surrey hills to mountains grew
In White of Selborne's loving view,—
He told how teal and loon he shot,
And how the eagle's eggs he got,
The feats on pond and river done,
The prodigies of rod and gun;
Till, warming with the tales he told,
Forgotten was the outside cold,
The bitter wind unheeded blew,
From ripening corn the pigeons flew,
The partridge drummed i' the wood, the mink
Went fishing down the river-brink.
In fields with bean or clover gay,
The woodchuck, like a hermit gray,
Peered from the doorway of his cell;
The muskrat plied the mason's trade,
And tier by tier his mud-walls laid;

And from the shagbark overhead
The grizzled squirrel dropped his shell.

Next, the dear aunt, whose smile of cheer
And voice in dreams I see and hear,—
The sweetest woman ever Fate
Perverse denied a household mate,
Who, lonely, homeless, not the less
Found peace in love's unselfishness,
And welcome wheresoe'er she went,
A calm and gracious element,
Whose presence seemed the sweet income
And womanly atmosphere of home,—
Called up her girlhood memories,
The huskings and the apple-bees,
The sleigh-rides and the summer sails,
Weaving through all the poor details
And homespun warp of circumstance
A golden woof-thread of romance.

For well she kept her genial mood
And simple faith of maidenhood;
Before her still a cloud-land lay,
The mirage loomed across her way;
The morning dew, that dries so soon
With others, glistened at her noon;
Through years of toil and soil and care
From glossy tress to thin gray hair,
All unprofaned she held apart
The virgin fancies of the heart.
Be shame to him of woman born
Who hath for such but thought of scorn.
There, too, our elder sister plied
Her evening task the stand beside;
A full, rich nature, free to trust,
Truthful and almost sternly just,
Impulsive, earnest, prompt to act,
And make her generous thought a fact,
Keeping with many a light disguise

The secret of self-sacrifice.
O heart sore-tried! thou hast the best
That Heaven itself could give thee,—rest,
Rest from all bitter thoughts and things!
    How many a poor one's blessing went
    With thee beneath the low green tent
Whose curtain never outward swings!

As one who held herself a part
Of all she saw, and let her heart
    Against the household bosom lean,
Upon the motley-braided mat
Our youngest and our dearest sat,
Lifting her large, sweet, asking eyes,
    Now bathed within the fadeless green
And holy peace of Paradise.
O, looking from some heavenly hill,
    Or from the shade of saintly palms,
    Or silver reach of river calms,

Do those large eyes behold me still?
With me one little year ago :—
The chill weight of the winter snow
   For months upon her grave has lain ;
And now, when summer south-winds blow
   And brier and harebell bloom again,
I tread the pleasant paths we trod,
I see the violet-sprinkled sod
Whereon she leaned, too frail and weak
The hillside flowers she loved to seek,
Yet following me where'er I went
With dark eyes full of love's content.
The birds are glad ; the brier-rose fills
The air with sweetness ; all the hills
Stretch green to June's unclouded sky ;
But still I wait with ear and eye
For something gone which should be nigh,
A loss in all familiar things,
In flower that blooms, and bird that sings.

And yet, dear heart ! remembering thee,
  Am I not richer than of old?
Safe in thy immortality,
  What change can reach the wealth I hold?
  What chance can mar the pearl and gold
Thy love hath left in trust with me?
And while in life's late afternoon,
  Where cool and long the shadows grow,
I walk to meet the night that soon
  Shall shape and shadow overflow,
I cannot feel that thou art far,
Since near at need the angels are ;
And when the sunset gates unbar,
  Shall I not see thee waiting stand,
And, white against the evening star,
  The welcome of thy beckoning hand ?

Brisk wielder of the birch and rule,
The master of the district school

Held at the fire his favored place,
Its warm glow lit a laughing face
Fresh-hued and fair, where scarce appeared
The uncertain prophecy of beard.
He teased the mitten-blinded cat,
Played cross-pins on my uncle's hat,
Sang songs, and told us what befalls
In classic Dartmouth's college halls.
Born the wild Northern hills among,
From whence his yeoman father wrung
By patient toil subsistence scant,
Not competence and yet not want,
He early gained the power to pay
His cheerful, self-reliant way ;
Could doff at ease his scholar's gown
To peddle wares from town to town ;
Or through the long vacation's reach
In lonely lowland districts teach,
Where all the droll experience found

At stranger hearths in boarding round,
The moonlit skater's keen delight,
The sleigh-drive through the frosty night.
The rustic party, with its rough
Accompaniment of blind-man's-buff,
And whirling plate, and forfeits paid,
His winter task a pastime made.
Happy the snow-locked homes wherein
He tuned his merry violin,
Or played the athlete in the barn,
Or held the good dame's winding yarn,
Or mirth-provoking versions told
Of classic legends rare and old,
Wherein the scenes of Greece and Rome
Had all the commonplace of home,
And little seemed at best the odds
'Twixt Yankee pedlers and old gods;
Where Pindus-born Araxes took
The guise of any grist-mill brook,

And dread Olympus at his will
Became a huckleberry hill.

A careless boy that night he seemed;
    But at his desk he had the look
And air of one who wisely schemed,
    And hostage from the future took
    In trainéd thought and lore of book.
Large-brained, clear-eyed,—of such as he
Shall Freedom's young apostles be,
Who, following in War's bloody trail,
Shall every lingering wrong assail;
All chains from limb and spirit strike,
Uplift the black and white alike;
Scatter before their swift advance
The darkness and the ignorance,
The pride, the lust, the squalid sloth,
Which nurtured Treason's monstrous growth,
Made murder pastime, and the hell

Of prison-torture possible ;
The cruel lie of caste refute,
Old forms remould, and substitute
For Slavery's lash the freeman's will,
For blind routine, wise-handed skill ;
A school-house plant on every hill,
Stretching in radiate nerve-lines thence
The quick wires of intelligence ;
Till North and South together brought
Shall own the same electric thought,
In peace a common flag salute,
And, side by side in labor's free
And unresentful rivalry,
Harvest the fields wherein they fought.

Another guest that winter night
Flashed back from lustrous eyes the light.
Unmarked by time, and yet not young,
The honeyed music of her tongue

And words of meekness scarcely told
A nature passionate and bold,
Strong, self-concentred, spurning guide,
Its milder features dwarfed beside
Her unbent will's majestic pride.
She sat among us, at the best,
A not unfeared, half-welcome guest,
Rebuking with her cultured phrase
Our homeliness of words and ways.
A certain pard-like, treacherous grace
 Swayed the lithe limbs and drooped the
  lash,
 Lent the white teeth their dazzling flash ;
 And under low brows, black with night,
 Rayed out at times a dangerous light ;
The sharp heat-lightnings of her face
Presaging ill to him whom Fate
Condemned to share her love or hate.
A woman tropical, intense

In thought and act, in soul and sense,
She blended in a like degree
The vixen and the devotee,
Revealing with each freak or feint
    The temper of Petruchio's Kate,
The raptures of Siena's saint.
Her tapering hand and rounded wrist
Had facile power to form a fist;
The warm, dark languish of her eyes
Was never safe from wrath's surprise.
Brows saintly calm and lips devout
Knew every change of scowl and pout;
And the sweet voice had notes more high
And shrill for social battle cry.

Since then what old cathedral town
Has missed her pilgrim staff and gown,
What convent-gate has held its lock
Against the challenge of her knock!

Through Smyrna's plague-hushed thorough·
    fares,
Up sea-set Malta's rocky stairs,
Gray olive slopes of hills that hem
Thy tombs and shrines, Jerusalem,
Or startling on her desert throne
The crazy Queen of Lebanon
With claims fantastic as her own,
Her tireless feet have held their way;
And still, unrestful, bowed, and gray,
She watches under Eastern skies,
    With hope each day renewed and fresh,
    The Lord's quick coming in the flesh,
Whereof she dreams and prophesies !

Where'er her troubled path may be,
    The Lord's sweet pity with her go !
The outward wayward life we see,
    The hidden springs we may not know.

Nor is it given us to discern
   What threads the fatal sisters spun,
   Through what ancestral years has run
The sorrow with the woman born,
What forged her cruel chain of moods,
What set her feet in solitudes,
   And held the love within her mute,
What mingled madness in the blood,
   A life-long discord and annoy,
   Water of tears with oil of joy,
And hid within the folded bud
   Perversities of flower and fruit.
It is not ours to separate
The tangled skein of will and fate,
To show what metes and bounds should
    stand
Upon the soul's debatable land,
And between choice and Providence
Divide the circle of events;

But He who knows our frame is just,
 Merciful, and compassionate,
And full of sweet assurances
And hope for all the language is,
That He remembereth we are dust!

At last the great logs, crumbling low,
Sent out a dull and duller glow,
The bull's-eye watch that hung in view,
Ticking its weary circuit through,
Pointed with mutely-warning sign
Its black hand to the hour of nine.
That sign the pleasant circle broke:
My uncle ceased his pipe to smoke,
Knocked from its bowl the refuse gray
And laid it tenderly away,
Then roused himself to safely cover
The dull red brands with ashes over.
And while, with care, our mother laid

The work aside, her steps she stayed
One moment, seeking to express
Her grateful sense of happiness
For food and shelter, warmth and health,
And love's contentment more than wealth,
With simple wishes (not the weak,
Vain prayers which no fulfilment seek,
But such as warm the generous heart,
O'er-prompt to do with Heaven its part)
That none might lack, that bitter night,
For bread and clothing, warmth and light.

Within our beds awhile we heard
The wind that round the gables roared,
With now and then a ruder shock,
Which made our very bedsteads rock.
We heard the loosened clapboards tost,
The board-nails snapping in the frost;
And on us, through the unplastered wall,

Felt the light sifted snow-flakes fall.
But sleep stole on, as sleep will do
When hearts are light and life is new ;
Faint and more faint the murmurs grew,
Till in the summer-land of dreams
They softened to the sound of streams,
Low stir of leaves, and dip of oars,
And lapsing waves on quiet shores.

Next morn we wakened with the shout
Of merry voices high and clear ;
And saw the teamsters drawing near
To break the drifted highways out.
Down the long hillside treading slow
We saw the half-buried oxen go,
Shaking the snow from heads uptost,
Their straining nostrils white with frost.
Before our door the straggling train
Drew up, an added team to gain.

The elders threshed their hands a-cold,
   Passed, with the cider-mug, their jokes
   From lip to lip ; the younger folks
Down   the   loose   snow-banks,   wrestling,
   rolled,
Then toiled again the cavalcade
   O'er windy hill, through clogged ravine,
   And woodland paths that wound between
Low drooping pine-boughs winter-weighed.
From every barn a team afoot,
At every house a new recruit,
Where, drawn by Nature's subtlest law,
Haply the watchful young men saw
Sweet doorway pictures of the curls
And curious eyes of merry girls,
Lifting their hands in mock defence
Against the snow-ball's compliments,
And reading in each missive tost
The charm with Eden never lost.

We heard once more the sleigh-bells' sound;
 And, following where the teamsters led,
The wise old Doctor went his round,
Just pausing at our door to say,
In the brief autocratic way
Of one who, prompt at Duty's call,
Was free to urge her claim on all,
 That some poor neighbor sick abed
At night our mother's aid would need.
For, one in generous thought and deed,
 What mattered in the sufferer's sight
 The Quaker matron's inward light,
The Doctor's mail of Calvin's creed?
All hearts confess the saints elect
 Who, twain in faith, in love agree,
And melt not in an acid sect
 The Christian pearl of charity!

So days went on: a week had passed

Since the great world was heard from last.

The Almanac we studied o'er,

Read and reread our little store,

Of books and pamphlets, scarce a score ;

One harmless novel, mostly hid

From younger eyes, a book forbid,

And poetry, (or good or bad,

A single book was all we had,)

Where Ellwood's meek, drab-skirted Muse,

   A stranger to the heathen Nine,

   Sang, with a somewhat nasal whine,

The wars of David and the Jews.

At last the floundering carrier bore

The village paper to our door.

Lo ! broadening outward as we read,

To warmer zones the horizon spread ;

In panoramic length unrolled

We saw the marvels that it told.

Before us passed the painted Creeks,

And daft McGregor on his raids
In Costa Rica's everglades.
And up Taygetos winding slow
Rode Ypsilanti's Mainote Greeks,
A Turk's head at each saddle-bow !
Welcome to us its week-old news,
Its corner for the rustic Muse,
Its monthly gauge of snow and rain,
Its record, mingling in a breath
The wedding knell and dirge of death ;
Jest, anecdote, and love-lorn tale,
The latest culprit sent to jail ;
Its hue and cry of stolen and lost,
Its vendue sales and goods at cost,
And traffic calling loud for gain.
We felt the stir of hall and street,
The pulse of life that round us beat ,
The chill embargo of the snow
Was melted in the genial glow ;

Wide swung again our ice-locked door,
And all the world was ours once more!

Clasp, Angel of the backward look
    And folded wings of ashen gray
    And voice of echoes far away,
The brazen covers of thy book;
The weird palimpsest old and vast,
Wherein thou hid'st the spectral past;
Where, closely mingling, pale and glow
The characters of joy and woe;
The monographs of outlived years,
Or smile-illumed or dim with tears,
    Green hills of life that slope to death,
And haunts of home, whose vistaed trees
Shade off to mournful cypresses
    With the white amaranths underneath.
Even while I look, I can but heed
    The restless sands' incessant fall,

Importunate hours that hours succeed,
Each clamorous with its own sharp need,
   And duty keeping pace with all.
Shut down and clasp the heavy lids ;
I hear again the voice that bids
The dreamer leave his dream midway
For larger hopes and graver fears :
Life greatens in these later years,
The century's aloe flowers to-day !

Yet, haply, in some lull of life,
Some Truce of God which breaks its strife,
The worlding's eyes shall gather dew,
   Dreaming in throngful city ways
Of winter joys his boyhood knew ;
And dear and early friends—the few
Who yet remain—shall pause to view
   These Flemish pictures of old days ;
Sit with me by the homestead hearth,

And stretch the hands of memory forth
  To warm them at the wood-fire's blaze!
And thanks untraced to lips unknown
Shall greet me like the odors blown
From unseen meadows newly mown,
Or lilies floating in some pond,
Wood-fringed, the wayside gaze beyond;
The traveller owns the grateful sense
Of sweetness near, he knows not whence,
And, pausing, takes with forehead bare
The benediction of the air.

MIRIAM.

MIRIAM.

One Sabbath day my friend and I
After the meeting, quietly
Passed from the crowded village lanes,
White with dry dust for lack of rains,
And climbed the neighboring slope, with
     feet
Slackened and heavy from the heat,
Although the day was wellnigh done,
And the low angle of the sun
Along the naked hillside cast
Our shadows as of giants vast.
We reached, at length, the topmost swell,
Whence, either way, the green turf fell
In terraces of nature down

To fruit-hung orchards, and the town
With white, pretenceless houses, tall
Church-steeples, and, o'ershadowing all,
Huge mills whose windows had the look
Of eager eyes that ill could brook
The Sabbath rest.   We traced the track
Of the sea-seeking river back
Glistening for miles above its mouth,
Through the long valley to the south.
And, looking eastward, cool to view,
Stretched the illimitable blue
Of ocean, from its curved coast-line ;
Sombred and still, the warm sunshine
Filled with pale gold-dust all the reach
Of slumberous woods from hill to beach,—
Slanted on walls of thronged retreats
From city toil and dusty streets,
On grassy bluff, and dune of sand,
And rocky island miles from land ;

Touched the tar-glancing sails, and showed
White lines of foam where long waves flowed
Dumb in the distance. In the north,
Dim through their misty hair, looked forth
The space-dwarfed mountains to the sea,
From mystery to mystery !

So, sitting on that green hill-slope,
We talked of human life, its hope
And fear, and unsolved doubts, and what
It might have been, and yet was not.
And, when at last the evening air
Grew sweeter for the bells of prayer
Ringing in steeples far below,
We watched the people churchward go,
Each to his place, as if thereon
The true shekinah only shone ;
And my friend queried how it came
To pass that they who owned the same

Great Master still could not agree
To worship Him in company.
Then, broadening in his thought, he ran
Over the whole vast field of man,—
The varying forms of faith and creed
That somehow served the holders' need;
In which, unquestioned, undenied,
Uncounted millions lived and died;
The bibles of the ancient folk,
Through which the heart of nations spoke;
The old moralities which lent
To home its sweetness and content,
And rendered possible to bear
The life of peoples everywhere
And asked if we, who boast of light,
Claim not a too exclusive right
To truths which must for all be meant,
Like rain and sunshine freely sent.
In bondage to the letter still.

We give it power to cramp and kill,—
To tax God's fulness with a scheme
Narrower than Peter's house-top dream,
His wisdom and his love with plans
Poor and inadequate as man's.
It must be that He witnesses
Somehow to all men that He is:
That something of His saving grace
Reaches the lowest of the race,
Who, through strange creed and rite, may
      draw
The hints of a diviner law.
We walk in clearer light;—but then,
Is He not God?—are they not men?
Are his responsibilities
For us alone and not for these?

And I made answer : " Truth is one;
And, in all lands beneath the sun,

Whoso hath eyes to see may see
The tokens of its unity.
No scroll of creed its fulness wraps,
We trace it not by school-boy maps,
Free as the sun and air it is
Of latitudes and boundaries.
In Vedic verse, in dull Koran,
Are messages of good to man ;
The angels to our Aryan sires
Talked by the earliest household fires ;
The prophets of the elder day,
The slant-eyed sages of Cathay,
Read not the riddle all amiss
Of higher life evolved from this.

"Nor doth it lessen what He taught,
Or make the gospel Jesus brought
Less precious, that His lips retold
Some portion of that truth of old ;

Denying not the proven seers,
The tested wisdom of the years ;
Confirming with his own impress
The common law of righteousness.
We search the world for truth ; we cull
The good, the pure, the beautiful
From graven stone and written scroll,
From all old flower-fields of the soul ;
And, weary seekers of the best,
We come back laden from our quest,
To find that all the sages said
Is in the Book our mothers read,
And all our treasure of old thought
In His harmonious fulness wrought
Who gathers in one sheaf complete
The scattered blades of God's sown wheat,
The common growth that maketh good
His all-embracing Fatherhood.

"Wherever through the ages rise
The altars of self-sacrifice,
Where love its arms has opened wide,
Or man for man has calmly died,
I see the same white wings outspread
That hovered o'er the Master's head!
Up from undated time they come,
The martyr souls of heathendom,
And to His cross and passion bring
Their fellowship of suffering.
I trace His presence in the blind
Pathetic gropings of my kind,—
In prayers from sin and sorrow wrung,
In cradle-hymns of life they sung,
Each, in its measure, but a part
Of the unmeasured Over-Heart;
And with a stronger faith confess
The greater that it owns the less.
Good cause it is for thankfulness

That the world-blessing of His life
With the long past is not at strife;
That the great marvel of His death
To the one order witnesseth,
No doubt of changeless goodness wakes,
No link of cause and sequence breaks,
But, one with nature, rooted is
In the eternal verities;
Whereby, while differing in degree
As finite from infinity,
The pain and loss for others borne,
Love's crown of suffering meekly worn,
The life man giveth for his friend
Become vicarious in the end;
Their healing place in nature take,
And make life sweeter for their sake.

" So welcome I from every source
The tokens of that primal Force,

Older than heaven itself, yet new
As the young heart it reaches to,
Beneath whose steady impulse rolls
The tidal wave of human souls;
Guide, comforter, and inward word,
The eternal spirit of the Lord!
Nor fear I aught that science brings
From searching through material things;
Content to let its glasses prove,
Not by the letter's oldness move.
The myriad worlds on worlds that course
The spaces of the universe;
Since everywhere the Spirit walks
The garden of the heart, and talks
With man, as under Eden's trees,
In all his varied languages.
Why mourn above some hopeless flaw
In the stone tables of the law,
When scripture every day afresh

Is traced on tablets of the flesh?
By inward sense, by outward signs,
God's presence still the heart divines;
Through deepest joy of Him we learn,
In sorest grief to Him we turn,
And reason stoops its pride to share
The child-like instinct of a prayer."

And then, as is my wont, I told
A story of the days of old,
Not found in printed books,—in sooth,
I fancy, with slight hint of truth,
Showing how differing faiths agree
In one sweet law of charity.
Meanwhile the sky had golden grown,
Our faces in its glory shone;
But shadows down the valley swept,
And gray below the ocean slept,
As time and space I wandered o'er

To tread the Mogul's marble floor,
And see a fairer sunset fall
On Jumna's wave and Agra's wall.

THE good Shah Akbar (peace be his al-
        way !)
Came forth from the Divan at close of day
Bowed with his burden of his many cares,
Worn with the hearing of unnumbered
        prayers,—
Wild cries for justice, the importunate
Appeals of greed and jealousy and hate,
And all the strife of sect and creed and rite,
Santon and Gouroo waging holy fight :
For the wise monarch, claiming not to be
Allah's avenger, left his people free,
With a faint hope, his Book scarce justified,
That all the paths of faith, though severed
        wide,

O'er which the feet of playful reverence
    passed,
Met at the gate of Paradise at last.

  He sought an alcove of his cool hareem,
Where, far beneath, he heard the Jumna's
    stream
Lapse soft and low along his palace wall,
And all about the cool sound of the fall
Of fountains, and of water circling free
Through marble ducts along the balcony;
The voice of women in the distance sweet,
And, sweeter still, of one who, at his feet,
Soothed his tired ear with songs of a far
    land
Where Tagus shatters on the salt sea-sand
The mirror of its cork-grown hills of drouth
And vales of vine, at Lisbon's harbor-
    mouth.

The date-palm rustled not; the peepul
    laid
Its topmost boughs against the balustrade,
Motionless as the mimic leaves and vines
That, light and graceful as the shawl-
    designs
Of Delhi or Umritsir, twined in stone ;
And the tired monarch, who aside had
    thrown
The day's hard burden, sat from care apart,
And let the quiet steal into his heart
From the still hour.   Below him Agra slept,
By the long light of sunset overswept :
The river flowing through a level land,
By mango-groves and banks of yellow sand,
Skirted with lime and orange, gay kiosks,
Fountains at play, tall minarets of mosques,
Fair pleasure-gardens, with their flowering
    trees

Relieved against the mournful cypresses ;
And, air-poised lightly as the blown sea-
      foam,
The marble wonder of some holy dome
Hung a white moonrise over the still wood,
Glassing its beauty in a stiller flood.

  Silent the monarch gazed, until the night
Swift-falling hid the city from his sight,
Then to the woman at his feet he said :
" Tell me, O Miriam, something thou hast
      read
In childhood of the Master of thy faith,
Whom Islam also owns. Our Prophet
      saith :
' He was a true apostle, yea,—a Word
And Spirit sent before me from the Lord.'
Thus the Book witnesseth ; and well I know
By what thou art, O dearest, it is so.

As the lute's tone the maker's hand be-
　　　trays,
The sweet disciple speaks her Master's
　　　praise."

　　Then Miriam, glad of heart, (for in some
　　　sort
She cherished in the Moslem's liberal court
The sweet traditions of a Christian child ;
And, through her life of sense, the unde-
　　　filed
And chaste ideal of the sinless One
Gazed on her with an eye she might not
　　　shun,—
The sad, reproachful look of pity, born
Of love that hath no part in wrath or scorn,)
Began, with low voice and moist eyes, to
　　　tell
Of the all-loving Christ, and what befell

When the fierce zealots, thirsting for her
    blood,
Dragged to his feet a shame of womanhood.
How, when his searching answer pierced
    within
Each heart, and touched the secret of its sin,
And her accusers fled his face before,
He bade the poor one go and sin no more.
And Akbar said, after a moment's thought,
" Wise is the lesson by thy prophet taught ;
Woe unto him who judges and forgets
What hidden evil his own heart besets !
Something of this large charity I find
In all the sects that sever human kind ;
I would to Allah that their lives agreed
More nearly with the lesson of their creed !
Those yellow Lamas who at Meerut pray
By wind and water power, and love to say :
' He who forgiveth not shall, unforgiven,

Fail of the rest of Buddha,' and who even
Spare the black gnat that stings them, vex
     my ears
With the poor hates and jealousies and fears
Nursed in their human hives. That lean,
     fierce priest
Of thy own people, (be his heart increased
By Allah's love!) his black robes smelling
     yet
Of Goa's roasted Jews, have I not met
Meek-faced, barefooted, crying in the street
The saying of his prophet true and sweet,—
' He who is merciful shall mercy meet ! ' "

  But, next day, so it chanced, as night
     began
To fall, a murmur through the hareem ran
That one, recalling in her dusky face
The full-lipped, mild-eyed beauty of a race

Known as the blameless Ethiops of Greek
    song,
Plotting to do her royal master wrong,
Watching, reproachful of the lingering light,
The evening shadows deepened for her flight,
Love-guided, to her home in a far land,
Now waited death at the great Shah's com-
    mand.

 Shapely as that dark princess for whose
    smile
A world was bartered, daughter of the Nile
Herself, and veiling in her large, soft eyes
The passion and the languor of her skies,
The Abyssinian knelt low at the feet
Of her stern lord: "O king, if it be meet,
And for thy honor's sake," she said, "that I,
Who am the humblest of thy slaves, should
    die,

I will not tax thy mercy to forgive.

Easier it is to die than to outlive

All that life gave me,—him whose wrong of
        thee

Was but the outcome of his love for me,

Cherished from childhood, when, beneath
        the shade

Of templed Axum, side by side we played.

Stolen from his arms, my lover followed me

Through weary seasons over land and sea ;

And two days since, sitting disconsolate

Within the shadow of the hareem gate,

Suddenly, as if dropping from the sky,

Down from the lattice of the balcony

Fell the sweet song by Tigre's cowherds
        sung

In the old music of his native tongue.

He knew my voice, for love is quick of ear,

Answering in song.

This night he waited near

To fly with me.   The fault was mine alone :

He knew thee not, he did but seek his own ;

Who, in the very shadow of thy throne,

Sharing thy bounty, knowing all thou art,

Greatest and best of men, and in her heart

Grateful to tears for favor undeserved,

Turned ever homeward, nor one moment
        swerved

From her young love.   He looked into my
        eyes,

He heard my voice, and could not otherwise

Than he hath done ; yet, save one wild
        embrace

When first we stood together face to face,

And all that fate had done since last we met

Seemed but a dream that left us children yet,

He hath not wronged thee nor thy royal
        bed ;

Spare him, O king! and slay me in his
    stead!"

  But over Akbar's brows the frown hung
    black,
And, turning to the eunuch at his back,
" Take them," he said, " and let the Jumna's
    waves
Hide both my shame and these accursed
    slaves !"
His loathly length the unsexed bondman
    bowed :
" On my head be it !"
                Straightway from a cloud
Of dainty shawls and veils of woven mist
The Christian Miriam rose, and, stooping,
    kissed
The monarch's hand. Loose down her
    shoulders bare

Swept all the rippled darkness of her hair,
Veiling the bosom that, with high, quick
    swell
Of fear and pity, through it rose and fell.

"Alas!" she cried, "hast thou forgotten
    quite
The words of Him we spake of yesternight?
Or thy own prophet's,—'Whoso doth endure
And pardon, of eternal life is sure?'
O great and good! be thy revenge alone
Felt in thy mercy to the erring shown;
Let thwarted love and youth their pardon
    plead,
Who sinned but in intent, and not in
    deed!"

One moment the strong frame of Akbar
    shook

With the great storm of passion.   Then his
    look
Softened to her uplifted face, that still
Pleaded more strongly than all words, until
Its pride and anger seemed like overblown,
Spent clouds of thunder left to tell alone
Of strife and overcoming.   With bowed
    head,
And smiting on his bosom : " God," he said,
" Alone is great, and let His holy name
Be honored, even to His servant's shame !
Well spake thy prophet, Miriam,—he alone
Who hath not sinned is meet to cast a stone
At such as these, who here their doom await,
Held like myself in the strong grasp of fate.
They sinned through love, as I through love
    forgive ;
Take them beyond my realm, but let them
    live ! "

And, like a chorus to the words of grace,
The ancient Fakir, sitting in his place,
Motionless as an idol and as grim,
In the pavilion Akbar built for him
Under the courtyard trees, (for he was
    wise,
Knew Menu's laws, and through his close-
    shut eyes
Saw things far off, and as an open book
Into the thoughts of other men could look,)
Began, half chant, half howling, to rehearse
The fragment of a holy Vedic verse;
And thus it ran: " He who all things for-
    gives
Conquers himself and all things else, and
    lives
Above the reach of wrong or hate or fear,
Calm as the gods, to whom he is most
    dear."

Two leagues from Agra still the traveller
    sees
The tomb of Akbar through its cypress-
    trees ;
And, near at hand, the marble walls that
    hide
The Christian Begum sleeping at his side.
And o'er her vault of burial (who shall tell
If it be chance alone or miracle ?)
The Mission press with tireless hand un-
    rolls
  The words of Jesus on it lettered
    Scrolls,—
Tells, in all tongues, the tale of mercy o'er,
And bids the guilty, "Go and sin no
    more ! "

It now was dew-fall ; very still
The night lay on the lonely hill,

Down which our homeward steps we bent,
And, silent, through great silence went,
Save that the tireless crickets played
Their long, monotonous serenade.
A young moon, at its narrowest,
Curved sharp against the darkening west;
And, momently, the beacon's star,
Slow wheeling o'er its rock afar,
From out the level darkness shot
One instant and again was not.
And then my friend spake quietly
The thought of both: " Yon crescent see!
Like Islam's symbol-moon it gives
Hints of the light whereby it lives:
Somewhat of goodness, something true
From sun and spirit shining through
All faiths, all worlds, as through the dark
Of ocean shines the lighthouse spark,
Attests the presence everywhere

Of love and providential care.
The faith the old Norse heart confessed
In one dear name,—the hopefulest
And tenderest heard from mortal lips
In pangs of birth or death, from ships
Ice-bitten in the winter sea,
Or lisped beside a mother's knee,—
The wiser world hath not outgrown,
And the All-Father is our own!

TENT ON THE BEACH.

THE TENT
ON THE BEACH.

WHEN heats as of a tropic clime
    Burned all our inland valleys through,
Three friends, the guests of summer time,
    Pitched their white tent where sea-
        winds blew.
Behind them, marshes, seamed and crossed
With narrow creeks, and flower-embossed,
Stretched to the dark oak wood, whose leafy
    arms
Screened from the stormy East the pleasant
    inland farms.

At full of tide their bolder shore
    Of sun-bleached sand the waters beat;

At ebb, a smooth and glistening floor
   They touched with light, receding feet.
Northward a green bluff broke the chain
Of sand-hills ; southward stretched a plain
Of salt grass, with a river winding down,
Sail-whitened, and beyond the steeples of the
   town,

Whence sometimes, when the wind was
   light
   And dull the thunder of the beach,
They heard the bell of morn and night
   Swing, miles away, their silver speech.
Above low scarp and turf-grown wall
They saw the fort flag rise and fall ;
And, the first star to signal twilight's
   hour,
The lamp-fire glimmer down from the tall
   light-house tower.

They rested there, escaped awhile
   From cares that wear the life away,
To eat the lotus of the Nile
   And drink the poppies of Cathay,—
To fling their loads of custom down,
  Like drift-weed, on the sand-slopes brown,
And in the sea waves drown the restless
      pack
Of duties, claims, and needs that barked
    upon their track.

One, with his beard scarce silvered, bore
   A ready credence in his looks,
A lettered magnate, lording o'er
   An ever-widening realm of books.
In him brain-currents, near and far,
Converged as in a Leyden jar ;
The old, dead authors thronged him round
    about,

And Elzevir's gray ghosts from leathern
    graves looked out.

He knew each living pundit well,
    Could weigh the gifts of him or her,
And well the market value tell
    Of poet and philosopher.
But if he lost, the scenes behind,
Somewhat of reverence vague and blind,
Finding the actors human at the best,
No readier lips than his the good he saw
    confessed.

His boyhood fancies not outgrown,
    He loved himself the singer's art ;
Tenderly, gently, by his own
    He knew and judged an author's heart.
No Rhadamanthine brow of doom.
Bowed the dazed pedant from his room ;

And bards, whose name is legion, if denied,
Bore off alike intact their verses and their
     pride.

Pleasant it was to roam about
    The lettered world as he had done,
And see the lords of song without
    Their singing robes and garlands on.
With Wordsworth paddle Rydal mere,
Taste rugged Elliott's home-brewed beer,
And with the ears of Rogers, at fourscore,
Hear Garrick's buskined tread and Walpole's
    wit once more.

And one there was, a dreamer born,
    Who, with a mission to fulfill,
Had left the Muses' haunts to turn
    The crank of an opinion-mill,
Making his rustic reed of song

A weapon in the war with wrong,
Yoking his fancy to the breaking-plough
That beam-deep turned the soil for truth to
        spring and grow.

Too quiet seemed the man to ride
    The winged Hippogriff Reform ;
Was his a voice from side to side
    To pierce the tumult of the storm ?
A silent, shy, peace-loving man,
He seemed no fiery partisan
To hold his way against the public frown,
The ban of Church and State, the fierce
    mob's hounding down.

For while he wrought with strenuous will
    The work his hands had found to do,
He heard the fitful music still
    Of winds that out of dream-land blew.

The din about him could not drown
What the strange voices whispered down;
Along his task-field weird processions swept,
The visionary pomp of stately phantoms
    stepped.

The common air was thick with dreams,—
    He told them to the toiling crowd;
Such music as the woods and streams
    Sang in his ear he sang aloud;
In still, shut bays, on windy capes,
He heard the call of beckoning shapes,
And, as the gray old shadows prompted him,
To homely moulds of rhyme he shaped their
    legends grim.

He rested now his weary hands,
    And lightly moralized and laughed,
As, tracing on the shifting sands

A burlesque of his paper-craft,
He saw the careless waves o'errun
His words, as time before had done,
Each day's tide-water washing clean away,
Like letters from the sand, the work of
yesterday.

And one, whose Arab face was tanned
By tropic sun and boreal frost,
So travelled there was scarce a land
Or people left him to exhaust,
In idling mood had from him hurled
The poor squeezed orange of the world,
And in the tent-shade, as beneath a palm,
Smoked, cross-legged like a Turk, in Ori-
ental calm.

The very waves that washed the sand
Below him, he had seen before

Whitening the Scandinavian strand
  And sultry Mauritanian shore.
From ice-rimmed isles, from summer seas
Palm-fringed, they bore him messages ;
He heard the plaintive Nubian songs
      again,
And mule-bells tinkling down the mountain-
      paths of Spain.

His memory round the ransacked earth
  On Ariel's girdle slid at ease ;
And, instant, to the valley's girth
  Of mountains, spice isles of the seas,
Faith flowered in minster stones, Art's
      guess
At truth and beauty, found access ;
Yet loved the while, that free cosmopolite,
Old friends, old ways, and kept his boy-
      hood's dreams in sight.

Untouched as yet by wealth and pride,
  That virgin innocence of beach :
No shingly monster, hundred-eyed,
  Stared its gray sand-birds out of reach ;
Unhoused, save where, at intervals,
  The white tents showed their canvas
    walls,
Where brief sojourners, in the cool, soft air,
Forgot their inland heats, hard toil, and
    year-long care.

Sometimes along the wheel-deep sand
  A one-horse wagon slowly crawled,
Deep laden with a youthful band,
  Whose look some homestead old re-
    called ;
Brother perchance, and sisters twain,
  And one whose blue eyes told, more plain
Than the free language of her rosy lip,

Of the still dearer claim of love's relation-
        ship.

With cheeks of russet-orchard tint,
    The light laugh of their native rills,
The perfume of their garden's mint,
    The breezy freedom of the hills,
They bore, in unrestrained delight,
The motto of the Garter's knight,
Careless as if from every gazing thing
Hid by their innocence, as Gyges by his
        ring.

The clanging sea-fowl came and went,
    The hunter's gun in the marshes rang;
At nightfall from a neighboring tent
    A flute-voiced woman sweetly sang.
Loose-haired, barefooted, hand in hand,
Young girls went tripping down the sand;

And youths and maidens, sitting in the
    moon,
Dreamed o'er the old fond dream from
    which we wake too soon.

At times their fishing-lines they plied,
    With an old Triton at the oar,
Salt as the sea-winds, tough and dried
    As a lean cusk from Labrador.
Strange tales he told of wreck and storm,—
Had seen the sea-snake's awful form,
And heard the ghosts on Haley's Isle com-
    plain,
Speak him off shore, and beg a passage to
    old Spain !

And there, on breezy morns, they saw
    The fishing-schooners outward run,
Their low-bent sails in tack and flaw

Turned white or dark to shade and sun.
Sometimes, in calms of closing day,
They watched the spectral mirage play,
Saw low, far islands looming tall and nigh,
And ships, with upturned keels, sail like a
    sea the sky.

Sometimes a cloud, with thunder black,
    Stooped low upon the darkening main.
Piercing the waves along its track
    With the slant javelins of rain.
And when west-wind and sunshine warm
Chased out to sea its wrecks of storm,
They saw the prismy hues in thin spray
    showers
Where the green buds of waves burst into
    white froth flowers.

And when along the line of shore
    The mists crept upward chill and damp,

Stretched, careless, on their sandy floor
    Beneath the flaring lantern lamp,
They talked of all things old and new,
Read, slept, and dreamed as idlers do ;
And in the unquestioned freedom of the
        tent,
Body and o'er-taxed mind to healthful ease
    unbent.

Once, when the sunset splendors died,
    And, trampling up the sloping sand,
In lines outreaching far and wide,
    The white-maned billows swept to
        land,
Dim seen across the gathering shade,
A vast and ghostly cavalcade,
They sat around their lighted kerosene,
Hearing the deep bass roar their every pause
    between.

Then, urged thereto, the Editor
  Within his full portfolio dipped,
Feigning excuse while searching for
  (With secret pride) his manuscript.
His pale face flushed from eye to beard,
  With nervous cough his throat he cleared,
And, in a voice so tremulous it betrayed
The anxious fondness of an author's heart,
    he read :

THE WRECK OF RIVERMOUTH.

RIVERMOUTH Rocks are fair to see
  By dawn or sunset shone across,
When the ebb of the sea has left them free,
  To dry their fringes of gold-green moss :
For there the river comes winding down
From salt sea-meadows and uplands brown
And waves on the outer rocks afoam
Shout to its waters, " Welcome home ! "

And fair are the sunny isles in view
   East of the grisly Head of the Boar,
And Agamenticus lifts its blue
   Disk of a cloud the woodlands o'er ;
And southerly, when the tide is down,
'Twixt white sea-waves and sand-hills brown,
The beach-birds dance and the gray gulls
      wheel
Over a floor of burnished steel.

Once, in the old Colonial days,
   Two hundred years ago or more,
A boat sailed down through the winding
     ways
   Of Hampton River to that low shore,
Full of a goodly company
Sailing out on the summer sea,
Veering to catch the land-breeze light,
With the Boar to left and the Rocks to right.

In Hampton meadows, where mowers laid
   Their scythes to the swaths of salted grass,
" Ah, well-a-day ! our hay must be made !"
   A young man sighed, who saw them pass.
Loud laughed his fellows to see him stand
Whetting his scythe with a listless hand,
Hearing a voice in a far-off song,
Watching a white hand beckoning long.

" Fie on the witch !" cried a merry girl.
   As they rounded the point where Goody
     Cole
Sat by her door with her wheel atwhirl,
   A bent and blear-eyed poor old soul.
" Oho !" she muttered, " ye 're brave to-
     day !
But I hear the little waves laugh and say,
' The broth will be cold that waits at home ;
For it's one to go, and another to come !' "

" She's cursed," said the skipper; " speak
     her fair :
   I'm scary always to see her shake
Her wicked head, with its wild gray hair,
   And nose like a hawk, and eyes like a
     snake."
But merrily still, with laugh and shout,
From Hampton River the boat sailed out,
Till the huts and the flakes on Star seemed
     nigh,
And they lost the scent of the pines of Rye.

They dropped their lines in the lazy tide,
   Drawing up haddock and mottled cod ;
They saw not the shadow that walked be-
     side,
   They heard not the feet with silence shod.
But thicker and thicker a hot mist grew,
Shot by the lightnings through and through ;

And muffled growls, like the growl of a
     beast,
Ran along the sky from west to east.

Then the skipper looked from the darkening
     sea
  Up to the dim and wading sun ;
But he spake like a brave man cheerily,
  " Yet there is time for our homeward run."
Veering and tacking, they backward wore ;
And just as a breath from the woods ashore
Blew out to whisper of danger past,
The wrath of the storm came down at last !

The skipper hauled at the heavy sail :
  " God be our help ! " he only cried,
As the roaring gale, like the stroke of a
     flail,
  Smote the boat on its starboard side.

The Shoalsmen looked, but saw alone
Dark films of rain-cloud slantwise blown,
Wild rocks up by the lightning's glare,
The strife and torment of sea and air.

Goody Cole looked out from her door;
    The Isles of Shoals were drowned and
        gone,
Scarcely she saw the Head of the Boar
    Toss the foam from tusks of stone.
She clasped her hands with a grip of pain,
The tear on her cheek was not of rain:
"They are lost," she muttered, "boat and
    crew!
Lord, forgive me! my words were true!"

Suddenly seaward swept the squall;
    The low sun smote through cloudy rack;
The shoals stood clear in the light, and all

The trend of the coast lay hard and black.
But far and wide as eye could reach,
No life was seen upon wave or beach;
The boat that went out at morning never
Sailed back again into Hampton River.

O mower, lean on thy bended snath,
    Look from the meadows green and low:
The wind of the sea is a waft of death,
    The waves are singing a song of woe!
By silent river, by moaning sea,
Long and vain shall thy watching be:
Never again shall thy sweet voice call,
Never the white hand rise and fall!

O Rivermouth Rocks, how sad a sight
    Ye saw in the light of breaking day!
Dead faces looking up cold and white
    From sand and sea-weed where they lay.

The mad old witch-wife wailed and wept,
And cursed the tide as it backward crept:
" Crawl back, crawl back, blue water-snake!
Leave your dead for the hearts that break!"

Solemn it was in that old day
   In Hampton town and its log-built
     church,
Where side by side the coffins lay
   And the mourners stood in aisle and
     porch.
In the singing-seats young eyes were dim,
The voices faltered that raised the hymn,
And Father Dalton, grave and stern,
Sobbed through his prayer and wept in turn.

But his ancient colleague did not pray,
   Because of his sin at fourscore years:
He stood apart, with the iron-gray

Of his strong brows knitted to hide his
    tears.
And a wretched woman, holding her breath
In the awful presence of sin and death,
Cowered and shrank, while her neighbors
    thronged
To look on the dead her shame had wronged.

Apart with them, like them forbid,
    Old Goody Cole looked drearily round,
As, two by two, with their faces hid,
    The mourners walked to the burying-
    ground.
She let the staff from her clasped hands fall:
" Lord, forgive us ! we 're sinners all ! "
And the voice of the old man answered her:
" Amen ! " said Father Bachiler.

So, as I sat upon Appledore
    In the calm of a closing summer day,

And the broken lines of Hampton shore
　　In purple mist of cloudland lay,
The Rivermouth Rocks their story told ;
And waves aglow with sunset gold,
Rising and breaking in steady chime,
Beat the rhythm and kept the time.

And the sunset paled, and warmed once
　　　more
　　With a softer, tenderer after-glow ;
In the east was moon-rise, with boats off-
　　　shore
　　And sails in the distance drifting slow.
The beacon glimmered from Portsmouth
　　· bar,
The White Isle kindled its great red star ;
And life and death in my old-time lay
Mingled in peace like the night and day !

"Well!" said the Man of Books, "your
    story
  Is not ill told in pleasant verse.
  As the Celt said of purgatory,
    One might go farther and fare worse."
  The reader smiled; and once again
  With steadier voice took up his strain,
While the fair singer from the neighboring
    tent
Drew near, and at his side a graceful listener
    bent.

THE GRAVE BY THE LAKE.

WHERE the Great Lake's sunny smiles
Dimple round its hundred isles,
And the mountain's granite ledge
Cleaves the water like a wedge,
Ringed about with smooth, gray stones,
Rest the giant's mighty bones.

Close beside, in shade and gleam,
  Laughs and ripples Melvin stream ;
Melvin water, mountain-born,
All fair flowers its banks adorn ;
All the woodland's voices meet,
Mingling with its murmurs sweet.

Over lowlands forest-grown,
Over waters island-strown,
  Over silver-sanded beach,
Leaf-locked bay and misty reach,
Melvin stream and burial-heap,
Watch and ward the mountains keep.
Who that Titan cromlech fills ?
Forest-kaiser, lord o' the hills ?
Knight who on the birchen tree
Carved his savage heraldry ?
Priest o' the pine-wood temples dim,
Prophet, sage, or wizard grim ?

Rugged type of primal man,
Grim utilitarian,
Loving woods for hunt and prowl,
Lake and hill for fish and fowl,
As the brown bear blind and dull
To the grand and beautiful :

Not for him the lesson drawn
From the mountains smit with dawn.
Star-rise, moon-rise, flowers of May,
Sunset's purple bloom of day,—
Took his life no hue from thence,
Poor amid such affluence ?

Haply unto hill and tree
All too near akin was he :
Unto him who stands afar
Nature's marvels greatest are ;
Who the mountain purple seeks
Must not climb the higher peaks.

Yet who knows in winter tramp,
Or the midnight of the camp,
What revealings faint and far,
Stealing down from moon and star,
Kindled in that human clod
Thought of destiny and God?

Stateliest forest patriarch,
Grand in robes of skin and bark,
What sepulchral mysteries,
What weird funeral-rites, were his?
What sharp wail, what drear lament,
Back scared wolf and eagle sent?

Now, whate'er he may have been,
Low he lies as other men;
On his mound the partridge drums,
There the noisy blue-jay comes;
Rank nor name nor pomp as he
In the grave's democracy.

Part thy blue lips, Northern lake !
Moss-grown rocks, your silence break !
Tell the tale, thou ancient tree !
Thou, too, slide-worn Ossipee !
Speak, and tell us how and when
Lived and died this king of men !

Wordless moans the ancient pine ;
Lake and mountain give no sign ;
Vain to trace this ring of stones ;
Vain the search of crumbling bones :
Deepest of all mysteries,
And the saddest, silence is.

Nameless, noteless, clay with clay
Mingles slowly day by day ;
But somewhere, for good or ill,
That dark soul is living still ;
Somewhere yet that atom's force
Moves the light-poised universe,

Strange that on his burial-sod
Harebells bloom, and golden-rod,
While the soul's dark horoscope
Holds no starry sign of hope !
Is the Unseen with sight at odds ?
Nature's pity more than God's ?

Thus I mused by Melvin side,
While the summer eventide
Made the woods and inland sea
And the mountains mystery ;
And the hush of earth and air
Seemed the pause before a prayer,—

Prayer for him, for all who rest,
Mother Earth, upon thy breast,—
Lapped on Christian turf, or hid
In rock-cave or pyramid :
All who sleep, as all who live,
Well may need the prayer, " Forgive ! "

Desert-smothered caravan,
Knee-deep dust that once was man,
Battle-trenches ghastly piled,
Ocean-floors with white bones tiled,
Crowded tomb and mounded sod,
Dumbly crave that prayer to God.

O the generations old
Over whom no church-bells tolled,
Christless, lifting up blind eyes
To the silence of the skies!
For the innumerable dead
Is my soul disquieted.

Where be now these silent hosts?
Where the camping-ground of ghosts?
Where the spectral conscripts led
To the white tents of the dead?
What strange shore or chartless sea
Holds the awful mystery?

Then the warm sky stooped to make
Double sunset in the lake ;
While above I saw with it,
Range on range, the mountains lit ;
And the calm and splendor stole
Like an answer to my soul.

Hear'st thou, O of little faith,
What to thee the mountain saith,
What is whispered by the trees ?—
" Cast on God thy care for these ;
Trust him, if thy sight be dim :
Doubt for them is doubt of Him.

" Blind must be their close-shut eyes
Where like night the sunshine lies,
Fiery-linked the self-forged chain
Binding ever sin to pain,
Strong their prison-house of will,
But without He waiteth still.

" Not with hatred's undertow
Doth the Love Eternal flow ;
Every chain that spirits wear
Crumbles in the breath of prayer ;
And the penitent's desire
Opens every gate of fire.

" Still Thy love, O Christ arisen,
Yearns to reach these souls in prison !
Through all depths of sin and loss
Drops the plummet of Thy cross !
Never yet abyss was found
Deeper than that cross could sound ! "

Therefore well may Nature keep
Equal faith with all who sleep,
Set her watch of hills around
Christian grave and heathen mound,
And to cairn and kirkyard send
Summer's flowery dividend.

Keep, O pleasant Melvin stream,
Thy sweet laugh in shade and gleam !
On the Indian's grassy tomb
Swing, O flowers, your bells of bloom !
Deep below, as high above,
Sweeps the circle of God's love.

———

He paused and questioned with his eye
    The hearers' verdict on his song.
A low voice asked : " Is 't well to pry
    Into the secrets which belong
Only to God ?—The life to be
Is still the unguessed mystery :
Unscaled, unpierced the cloudy walls remain,
We beat with dream and wish the soundless
        doors in vain.

" But faith beyond our sight may go."
    He said : " The gracious Fatherhood

Can only know above, below,
   Eternal purposes of good.
  From our free heritage of will,
  The bitter springs of pain and ill
Flow only in all worlds.   The perfect day
Of God is shadowless, and love is love
     always."

  " I know," she said, " the letter kills ;
   That on our arid fields of strife
  And heat of clashing texts distils
   The dew of spirit and of life.
  But, searching still the written Word,
  I fain would fine, Thus saith the Lord,
A voucher for the hope I also feel
That sin can give no wound beyond love's
     power to heal."

  " Pray," said the Man of Books, " give
    o'er

A theme too vast for time and place.
Go on, Sir Poet, ride once more
  Your hobby at his old free pace.
 But let him keep, with step discreet,
 The solid earth beneath his feet.
In the great mystery which around us lies,
The wisest is a fool, the fool Heaven helped
    is wise."

The Traveller said : " If songs have
    creeds,
  Their choice of them let singers make ;
But Art no other sanction needs
  Than beauty for its own fair sake,
 It grinds not in the mill of use,
 Nor asks for leave, nor begs excuse ;
It makes the flexile laws it deigns to own,
And gives its atmosphere its color and its
    tone.

"Confess, old friend, your austere school
  Has left your fancy little chance ;
You square to reason's rigid rule
  The flowing outlines of romance.
With conscience keen from exercise,
And chronic fear of compromise,
You check the free play of your rhymes, to
    clap
A moral underneath, and spring it like a
    trap."

The sweet voice answered : " Better so
  Than bolder flights that know no
    check ;
Better to use the bit, than throw
  The reins all loose on fancy's neck.
The liberal range of Art should be
The breadth of Christian liberty,
Restrained alone by challenge and alarm

Where its charmed footsteps tread the
  border land of harm.

 " Beyond the poet's day-dream lives
  The eternal epic of the man.
Be thanks to him who only gives,
  True to himself, the best he can.
Of narrow scope his verse may seem,
  But rippled lake and singing stream
Find fitting audience, in themselves com-
  plete
As the great sea that rolls its thunder at our
  feet.

 " In sight and sound, our rugged coast
  Shall tell of him from year to year,
Nor lightly shall the lays be lost
  That homely firesides love to bear.
For still on truth's and nature's tests

The common heart its verdict rests,
By simple instinct guided in its choice,
It loves the song that lends its own expe-
    rience voice."

Laughing, the Critic bowed.   " I yield
    The point without another word ;
Who ever yet a case appealed
    Where beauty's judgment had been
    heard ?
And you, my good friend, owe to me
Your warmest thanks for such a plea,
As true withal as sweet.   For my offence
Of cavil, let her praise be ample recom-
    pense."

Across the sea one large, low star,
    With crimson light that came and went,
Revolving on its tower afar,

Looked through the doorway of the
    tent.
While outward, over sand-slopes wet,
The lamp flashed down its yellow jet
On the long wash of waves, with red and
    green
Tangles of weltering weed through the
    white foam-wreaths seen.

" ' Sing while we may,—another day
    May bring enough of sorrow ; '—thus
Our Traveller in his own sweet lay,
    His Crimean camp-song, hints to us,"
The lady said.   " So let it be ;
Sing us a song," exclamed all three.
She smiled : " I can but marvel at your
    choice
To hear our poet's words through my poor
    borrowed voice."

Her window opens to the bay,
On glistening light or misty gray,
And there at dawn and set of day
    In prayer she kneels :
" Dear Lord ! " she said, " to many a
    home
From wind and wave the wanderers
    come ;
I only see the tossing foam
    Of stranger keels.

" Blown out and in by summer gales,
The stately ships, with crowded sails,
And sailors leaning o'er their rails,
    Before me glide ;
They come, they go, but nevermore,
Spice-laden from the Indian shore,
I see the swift-winged Isidore
    The waves divide.

" O Thou ! with whom the night is day
And one the near and far away,
Look out on yon gray waste, and say
   Where lingers he.
Alive, perchance, on some long beach
Or thirsty isle beyond the reach
Of man, he hears the mocking speech
   Of wind and sea.

" O dread and cruel deep, reveal
The secret which thy waves conceal,
And, ye wild sea-birds, hither wheel
   And tell your tale.
Let winds that tossed his raven hair
A message from my lost one bear,—
Some thought of me, a last fond prayer
   Or dying wail !

" Come, with your dreariest truth shut out
The fears that haunt me round about ;

O God ! I cannot bear this doubt
   That stifles breath.
The worst is better than the dread ;
Give me but leave to mourn my dead
Asleep in trust and hope, instead
   Of life in death ! ''

It might have been the evening breeze
That whispered in the garden trees,
It might have been the sound of seas
   That rose and fell ;
But, with her heart, if not her ear,
The old loved voice she seemed to hear :
" I wait to meet thee : be of cheer.
   For all is well ! ''

———

The sweet voice into silence went,
 While a low murmur of applause

From lip to lip ran round the tent;
And, after brief and fitting pause,
Glancing his written pages o'er,
The Reader tried his part once more;
Leaving the land of hackmatack and pine
For Tuscan valleys glad with olive and
with vine.

THE BROTHER OF MERCY.

PIERO LUCA, known of all the town
As the gray porter by the Pitti wall
Where the noon shadows of the gardens fall,
Sick and in dolor, waited to lay down
His last sad burden, and beside his mat
The barefoot monk of La Certosa sat.

Unseen, in square and blossoming garden
drifted,

Soft sunset lights through green Val d'
    Arno sifted ;
Unheard, below the living shuttles shifted
Backward and forth, and wove, in love or
    strife,
In mirth or pain, the mottled web of life :
But when at last came upward from the
    street
Tinkle of bell and tread of measured feet,
The sick man started, strove to rise in vain,
Sinking back heavily with a moan of pain.
And the monk said, " 'T is but the Brother-
    hood
Of Mercy going on some errand good :
Their black masks by the palace-wall I see."
Piero answered faintly, " Woe is me !
This day for the first time in forty years
In vain the bell hath sounded in my ears,
Calling me with my brethren of the mask,

Beggar and prince alike, to some new task
Of love or pity,—haply from the street
To bear a wretch plague-stricken, or, with
      feet
Hushed to the quickened ear and feverish
      brain,
To tread the crowded lazaretto's floors,
Down the long twilight of the corridors,
'Midst tossing arms and faces full of pain.
I loved the work : it was its own reward.
I never counted on it to offset
My sins, which are many, or make less my
      debt
To the free grace and mercy of our Lord ;
But somehow, father, it has come to be
In these long years so much a part of me,
I should not know myself, if lacking it,
But with the work the worker too would
      die,

And in my place some other self would sit
Joyful or sad,—what matters, if not I ?
And now all's over. Woe is me !"—" My
    son,"
The monk said soothingly, " thy work is
    done ;
And no more as a servant, but the guest
Of God thou enterest thy eternal rest.
No toil, no tears, no sorrow for the lost
Shall mar thy perfect bliss. Thou shalt sit
    down
Clad in white robes, and wear a golden crown
Forever and forever."—Piero tossed
On his sick pillow : " Miserable me !
I am too poor for such grand company ;
The crown would be too heavy for this gray
Old head ; and God forgive me if I say
It would be hard to sit there night and day,
Like an image in the Tribune, doing naught

With these hard hands, that all my life have
  wrought,
Not for bread only, but for pity's sake.
I'm dull at prayers : I could not keep
  awake
Counting my beads.   Mine's but a crazy
  head,
Scarce worth the saving, if all else be dead.
And if one goes to heaven without a heart,
God knows he leaves behind his better part.
I love my fellow-men ; the worst I know
I would do good to.   Will death change
  me so
That I shall sit among the lazy saints,
Turning a deaf ear to the sore complaints
Of souls that suffer ?   Why, I never yet
Left a poor dog in the *strada* hard beset,
Or ass o'erladen !   Must I rate man less
Than dog or ass, in holy selfishness ?

Methinks (Lord, pardon, if the thought be
    sin !)
The world of pain were better, if therein
One's heart might still be human, and de-
    sires
Of natural pity drop upon its fires
Some cooling tears."
               Thereat the pale monk crossed
His brow, and, muttering, " Madman ! thou
    art lost ! "
Took up his pyx and fled ; and, left alone,
The sick man closed his eyes with a great
    groan
That sank into a prayer, " Thy will be
    done ! "

Then was he made aware, by soul or ear,
Of somewhat pure and holy bending o'er
    him,

And of a voice like that of her who bore
      him,
Tender and most compassionate : " Never
      fear ! . . . .
For heaven is love, as God himself is love ;
Thy work below shall be thy work above."
And when he looked, lo ! in the stern monk's
      place
He saw the shining of an angel's face !

    The Traveller broke the pause. " I've
      seen
      The Brothers down the long street steal,
Back, silent, masked, the crowd between,
    And felt to doff my hat and kneel
With heart, if not with knee, in prayer,
For blessings on their pious care."
The Reader wiped his glasses : " Friends of
      mine,

We'll try our home-brewed next, instead of
　　foreign wine."

THE CHANGELING.

For the fairest maid in Hampton
　　They needed not to search,
Who saw young Anna Favor
　　Come walking into church,—

Or bringing from the meadows,
　　At set of harvest-day,
The frolic of the blackbirds,
　　The sweetness of the hay.

Now the weariest of all mothers,
　　The saddest two-years bride,
She scowls in the face of her husband,
　　And spurns her child aside.

" Rake out the red coals, goodman,—
　　For there the child shall lie,
Till the black witch comes to fetch her,
　　And both up chimney fly.

" It's never my own little daughter,
　　It's never my own," she said ;
" The witches have stolen my Anna,
　　And left me an imp instead.

" O, fair and sweet was my baby,
　　Blue eyes, and hair of gold ;
But this is ugly and wrinkled,
　　Cross, and cunning, and old.

" I hate the touch of her fingers,
　　I hate the feel of her skin ;
It's not the milk from my bosom,
　　But my blood, that she sucks in.

" My face grows sharp with the torment;
   Look! my arms are skin and bone! —
Rake open the red coals, goodman,
   And the witch shall have her own.

" She'll come when she hears it crying,
   In the shape of an owl or bat,
And she'll bring us our darling Anna
   In the place of her screeching brat."

Then the goodman, Ezra Dalton,
   Laid his hand upon her head:
" Thy sorrow is great, O woman!
   I sorrow with thee," he said.

" The paths to trouble are many,
   And never but one sure way
Leads out to the light beyond it:
   My poor wife, let us pray."

Then he said to the great All-Father,
   "Thy daughter is weak and blind;
Let her sight come back, and clothe her
   Once more in her right mind.

"Lead her out of this evil shadow,
   Out of these fancies wild;
Let the holy love of the mother
   Turn again to her child.

"Make her lips like the lips of Mary
   Kissing her blessed Son;
Let her hands, like the hands of Jesus,
   Rest on her little one.

"Comfort the soul of thy handmaid,
   Open her prison-door,
And thine shall be all the glory
   And praise forevermore."

Then into the face of its mother
    The baby looked up and smiled;
And the cloud of her soul was lifted,
    And she knew her little child.

A beam of the slant west sunshine
    Made the wan face almost fair,
Lit the blue eyes' patient wonder,
    And the rings of pale gold hair.

She kissed it on lip and forehead,
    She kissed it on cheek and chin,
And she bared her snow-white bosom
    To the lips so pale and thin.

O, fair on her bridal morning
    Was the maid who blushed and smiled,
But fairer to Ezra Dalton
    Looked the mother of his child.

With more than a lover's fondness
  He stooped to her worn young face,
And the nursing child and the mother
  He folded in one embrace.

"Blessed be God!" he murmured.
  "Blessed be God!" she said;
"For I see, who once was blinded,—
  I live, who once was dead.

"Now mount and ride, my goodman,
  As thou lovest thy own soul!
Woe's me, if my wicked fancies
  Be the death of Goody Cole!"

His horse he saddled and bridled,
  And into the night rode he,—
Now through the great black woodland,
  Now by the white-beached sea.

He rode through the silent clearings,
　　He came to the ferry wide,
And thrice he called to the boatman
　　Asleep on the other side.

He set his horse to the river.
　　He swam to Newbury town,
And he called up justice Sewall
　　In his nightcap and his gown.

And the grave and worshipful justice
　　(Upon whose soul be peace !)
Set his name on the jailer's warrant
　　For Goodwife Cole's release.

Then through the night the hoof-beats
　　Went sounding like a flail ;
And Goody Cole at cockcrow
　　Came forth from Ipswich jail.

———

"Here is a rhyme :—I hardly dare
    To venture on its theme worn out;
What seems so sweet by Doon and Ayr
    Sounds simply silly hereabout;
And pipes by lips Arcadian blown
Are only tin horns at our own.
Yet still the muse of pastoral walks with us,
While Hosea Biglow sings, our new The-
    ocritus."

THE MAIDS OF ATTITASH.

In sky and wave the white clouds swam,
And the blue hills of Nottingham
    Through gaps of leafy green
    Across the lake were seen,—

When, in the shadow of the ash
That dreams its dream in Attitash,
  In the warm summer weather,
  Two maidens sat together.

They sat and watched in idle mood
The gleam and shade of lake and wood,—
  The beach the keen light smote,
  The white sail of a boat,—

Swan flocks of lilies shoreward lying,
In sweetness, not in music, dying,—
  Hardhack, and Virgins-bower,
  And white-spiked clethra-flower.

With careless ears they heard the plash
And breezy wash of Attitash,
  The wood-bird's plaintive cry,
  The locust's sharp reply.

And teased the while, with playful hand,
The shaggy dog of Newfoundland.
   Whose uncouth frolic spilled
   Their baskets berry-filled.

Then one, the beauty of whose eyes
Was evermore a great surprise,
   Tossed back her queenly head,
   And, lightly laughing, said,—

"No bridegroom's hand be mine to hold
That is not lined with yellow gold;
   I tread no cottage floor;
   I own no lover poor.

"My love must come on silken wings,
With bridal lights of diamond rings,—
   Not foul with kitchen smirch,
   With tallow-dip for torch."

The other, on whose modest head
Was lesser dower of beauty shed,
  With look for home-hearths meet,
  And voice exceeding sweet,

Answered,—"We will not rivals be;
Take thou the gold, leave love to me;
  Mine be the cottage small,
  And thine the rich man's hall.

"I know, indeed, that wealth is good;
But lowly roof and simple food,
  With love that hath no doubt,
  Are more than gold without."

Hard by a farmer hale and young
His cradle in the rye-field swung,
  Tracking the yellow plain
  With windrows of ripe grain.

And still, whene'er he paused to whet
His scythe, the sidelong glance he met
  Of large dark eyes, where strove
  False pride and secret love.

Be strong, young mower of the grain;
That love shall overmatch disdain,
  Its instincts soon or late
  The heart shall vindicate.

In blouse of gray, with fishing rod,
Half screened by leaves, a stranger trod
  The margin of the pond,
  Watching the group beyond.

The supreme hours unnoted come;
Unfelt the turning tides of doom;
  And so the maids laughed on,
  Nor dreamed what Fate had done,—

Nor knew the step was Destiny's
That rustled in the birchen trees,
  As, with lives forecast,
  Fisher and mower passed.

Erelong by lake and rivulet side
The summer roses paled and died,
  And Autumn's fingers shed
  The maple's leaves of red.

Through the long gold-hazed afternoon,
Alone, but for the diving loon,
  The partridge in the brake,
  The black duck on the lake,

Beneath the shadow of the ash
Sat man and maid by Attitash;
  And earth and air made room
  For human hearts to bloom.

Soft spread the carpets of the sod,
And scarlet-oak and golden-rod
　　With blushes and with smiles
　　Lit up the forest aisles.

The mellow light the lake aslant,
The pebbled margin's ripple-chant
　　Attempered and low-toned,
　　The tender mystery owned.

And through the dream the lovers dreamed
Sweet sounds stole in and soft lights
　　　　streamed ;
　　The sunshine seemed to bless,
　　The air was a caress.

Not she who lightly laughed is there,
With scornful toss of midnight hair,
　　Her dark, disdainful eyes,
　　And proud lip worldly-wise.

Her haughty vow is still unsaid,
But all she dreamed and coveted
  Wears, half to her surprise,
  The youthful farmer's guise !

With more than all her old-time pride
She walks the rye-field at his side,
  Careless of cot of hall,
  Since love transfigures all.

Rich beyond dreams, the vantage-ground
Of life is gained ; her hands have found
  The talisman of old
  That changes all to gold.

While she who could for love dispense
With all its glittering accidents,
  And trust her heart alone,
  Finds love and gold her own.

What wealth can buy or art can build
Awaits her; but her cup is filled
    Even now unto the brim;
    Her world is love and him!

    The while he heard, the Book-man drew
      A length of make-believing face,
With   smothered   mischief   laughing
    through:
    "Why, you shall sit in Ramsay's place,
And, with his Gentle Shepherd, keep
On Yankee hills immortal sheep,
While love-lorn swains and maids the seas
    beyond
Hold dreamy tryst around your huckleberry-
    pond."

The Traveller laughed: "Sir Galahad
    Singing of love the Trouvere's lay!

How should he know the blindfold lad
   From one of Vulcan's forge-boys?"—
    "Nay,
He better sees who stands outside
Then they who in procession ride,"
The Reader answered: "Selectmen and
   squire
Miss, while they make, the show that way-
   side folks admire.

"Here is a wild tale of the North,
   Our travelled friend will own as one
Fit for a Norland Christmas hearth
   And lips of Christian Andersen.
They tell it in the valleys green
Of the fair island he has seen,
Low lying off the pleasant Swedish shore,
Washed by the Baltic Sea, and watched by
   Elsinore."

KALLUNDBORG CHURCH

" Tie stille, barn min!

Imorgen kommer Fin,

Fa'er din,

Og gi'er Esbern Snares öine og hjerte at lege
med ! "

Zealand Rhyme.

" BUILD at Kallundborg by the sea
A church as stately as church may be,
And there shalt thou wed my daughter fair,"
Said the Lord of Nesvek to Esbern Snare.

And the Baron laughed.   But Esbern said,
" Though I lose my soul, I will Helva
wed ! "
And off he strode, in his pride of will,
To the Troll who dwelt in Ulshoi hill.

" Build, O Troll, a church for me
At Kallundborg by the mighty sea;
Build it stately, and build it fair,
Build it quickly," said Esbern Snare.

But the sly Dwarf said, " No work is
        wrought
By Trolls of the Hills, O man, for naught.
What wilt thou give for thy church so fair ? "
" Set thy own price," quoth Esbern Snare.

" When Kallundborg church is builded well,
Thou must the name of its builder tell,
Or thy heart and thine eyes must be my
        boon."
" Build," said Esbern, " and build it soon."

By night and by day the Troll wrought on;
He hewed the timbers, he piled the stone;

But day by day, as the walls rose fair,
Darker and sadder grew Esbern Snare.

He listened by night, he watched by day,
He sought and thought, but he dared not
     pray ;
In vain he called on the Elle-maids shy,
And the Neck and the Nis gave no reply.

Of his evil bargain far and wide
A rumor ran through the country-side ;
And Helva of Nesvek, young and fair
Prayed for the soul of Esbern Snare.

And now the church was wellnigh done ;
One pillar it lacked, and one alone ;
And the grim Troll muttered, " Fool thou
     art !
To-morrow gives me thy eyes and heart ! "

By Kallundborg in black despair,
Through wood and meadow, walked Esbern
      Snare,
Till, worn and weary, the strong man sank
Under the birches on Ulshoi bank.

At his last day's work he heard the Troll
Hammer and delve in the quarry's hole;
Before him the church stood large and fair;
"I have builded my tomb," said Esbern
      Snare.

And he closed his eyes the sight to hide,
When he heard a light step at his side:
"O Esbern Snare!" a sweet voice said,
"Would I might die now in thy stead!"

With a grasp by love and by fear made
      strong,

He held her fast, and he held her long;
With the beating heart of a bird afeared,
She hid her face in his flame-red beard.

"O love!" he cried, "let me look to-day
In thine eyes ere mine are plucked away;
Let me hold thee close, let me feel thy
        heart
Ere mine by the Troll is torn apart!

"I sinned, O Helva, for love of thee!
Pray that the Lord Christ pardon me!"
But fast as she prayed, and faster still,
Hammered the Troll in Ulshoi hill.

He knew, as he wrought, that a loving heart
Was somehow baffling his evil art;
For more than spell or Elf or Troll
Is a maiden's prayer for her lover's soul.

And Esbern listened, and caught the sound
Of a Troll-wife singing underground:
" To-morrow comes Fine, father thine:
Lie still and hush thee, baby mine!

" Lie still, my darling! next sunrise
Thou'lt play with Esbern Snare's heart and
   eyes! "
" Ho! ho!" quoth Esbern, " is that your
   game?
Thanks to the Troll-wife, I know his
   name! "

The Troll he heard him, and hurried on
To Kallundborg church with the lacking
   stone.
" Too late, Gaffer Fine!" cried Esbern
   Snare;
And Troll and pillar vanished in air!

That night the harvesters heard the sound
Of a woman sobbing underground,
And the voice of the Hill-Troll loud with
    blame
Of the careless singer who told his name.

Of the Troll of the church they sing the
    rune
By the Northern Sea in the harvest moon ;
And the fishers of Zealand hear him still
Scolding his wife in Ulshoi hill.

And seaward over its groves of birch
Still looks the tower of Kallundborg church,
Where, first at its altar, a wedded pair,
Stood Helva of Nesvek and Esbern Snare !

———

"What," asked the Traveller, "would
    our sires,

The old Norse story-tellers, say
    Of sun-graved pictures, ocean wires,
        And smoking steamboats of to-day?
    And this, O, lady, by your leave,
        Recalls your song of yester eve:
Pray, let us have that Cable-hymn once
        more."
" Hear, hear ! " the Book-man cried, "the
        lady has the floor.

" These noisy waves below perhaps
        To such a strain will lend their ear,
    With softer voice and lighter lapse
        Come stealing up the sands to hear,
    And what they once refused to do
        For old King Knut accord to you.
Nay, even the fishes shall your listeners be,
As once, the legend runs, they heard St.
        Anthony.

O lonely bay of Trinity,
    O dreary shores, give ear!
Lean down unto the white-lipped sea
    The voice of God to hear!

From world to world his couriers fly,
    Thought-winged and shod with fire;
The angel of His stormy sky
    Rides down the sunken wire.

What saith the herald of the Lord?
    " The world's long strife is done;
Close wedded by that mystic cord,
    Its continents are one.

" And one in heart, as one in blood,
    Shall all her peoples he;
The hands of human brotherhood
    Are clasped beneath the sea.

" Through Orient seas, o'er Afric's plain
   And Asian mountains borne,
The vigor of the Northern brain
   Shall nerve the world outworn

" From clime to clime, from shore to shore,
   Shall thrill the magic thread ;
The new Prometheus steals once more
   The fire that wakes the dead."

Throb on, strong pulse of thunder ! beat
   From answering beach to beach ;
Fuse nations in thy kindly heat,
   And melt the chains of each !

Wild terror of the sky above,
   Glide tamed and dumb below !
Bear gently, Ocean's carrier-dove,
   Thy errands to and fro.

Weave on, swift shuttle of the Lord,
　　Beneath the deep so far,
The bridal robe of earth's accord,
　　The funeral shroud of war!

For lo! the fall of Ocean's wall
　　Space mocked and time outrun;
And round the world the thought of all
　　Is as the thought of one!

The poles unite, the zones agree,
　　The tongues of striving cease;
As on the Sea of Galilee
　　The Christ is whispering, " Peace!"

———

" Glad prophecy! to this at last,"
　　The Reader said, "shall all things
　　come.

Forgotten by the bugle's blast,
   And battle-music of the drum.
A little while the world may run
Its old mad way, with needle-gun
And iron-clad, but truth, at last, shall reign :
The cradle-song of Christ was never sung
   in vain ! ''

Shifting his scattered papers, " Here,"
   He said, as died the faint applause,
" Is something that I found last year
   Down on the island known as Orr's.
I had it from a fair-haired girl
Who, oddly, bore the name of Pearl,
(As if by some droll freak of circumstance,)
Classic, or wellnigh so, in Harriet Stowe's
   romance."

THE DEAD SHIP OF HARPSWELL.

WHAT flecks the outer gray beyond
    The sundown's golden trail?
The white flash of a sea-bird's wing,
    Or gleam of slanting sail?
Let young eyes watch from Neck and Point,
    And sea-worn elders pray,—
The ghost of what was once a ship
    Is sailing up the bay!

From gray sea-fog, from icy drift,
    From peril and from pain,
The home-bound fisher greets thy lights,
    O hundred-harbored Maine!
But many a keel shall seaward turn,
    And many a sail outstand,
When, tall and white, the Dead Ship looms
    Against the dusk of land.

She rounds the headland's bristling pines ;
　　She threads the isle-set bay ;
No spur of breeze can speed her on
　　Nor ebb of tide delay.
Old men still walk the Isle of Orr
　　Who tell ner date and name,
Old shipwrights sit in Freeport yards
　　Who hewed her oaken frame.

What weary doom of baffled quest,
　　Thou sad sea-ghost, is thine ?
What makes thee in the haunts of home
　　A wonder and a sign ?
No foot is on thy silent deck,
　　Upon thy helm no hand ;
No ripple hath the soundless wind
　　That smites thee from the land !

For never comes the ship to port,
　　Howe'er the breeze may be ;

Just when she nears the waiting shore
    She drifts again to sea.
No tack of sail, nor turn of helm,
    Nor sheer of veering side ;
Stern-fore she drives to sea and night,
    Against the wind and tide.

In vain o'er Harpswell Neck the star
    Of evening guides her in ;
In vain for her the lamps are lit
    Within thy tower, Seguin !
In vain the harbor-boat shall hail,
    In vain the pilot call ;
No hand shall reef her spectral sail,
    Or let her anchor fall.

Shake, brown old wives, with dreary joy,
    Your gray-head hints of ill ;
And, over sick-beds whispering low,

Your prophecies fulfil.
Some home amid yon birchen trees
    Shall drape its door with woe;
And slowly where the Dead Ship sails,
    The burial boat shall row!

From Wolf Neck and from Flying Point,
    From island and from main,
From sheltered cove and tided creek,
    Shall glide the funeral train.
The dead-boat with the bearers four,
    The mourners at her stern,—
And one shall go the silent way
    Who shall no more return!

And men shall sigh, and women weep,
    Whose dear ones pale and pine,
And sadly over sunset seas
    Await the ghostly sign.

They know not that its sails are filled
    By pity's tender breath,
Nor see the Angel at the helm
    Who steers the Ship of Death!

———

"Chill as a down-east breeze should be,"
    The Book-man said. "A ghostly touch
The legend has.   I'm glad to see
    Your flying Yankee beat the Dutch."
"Well, here is something of the sort
    Which one midsummer day I caught
In Narraganset Bay, for lack of fish,"
"We wait," the Traveller said; "serve hot
    or cold your dish."

THE PALATINE.

LEAGUES north, as fly the gull and auk,
Point Judith watches with eye of hawk ;
Leagues south, thy beacon flames, Montauk !

Lonely and wind-shorn, wood-forsaken,
With never a tree for Spring to waken,
For tryst of lovers or farewells taken,

Circled by waters that never freeze,
Beaten by billow and swept by breeze,
Lieth the island of Manisees,

Set at the mouth of the Sound to hold
The coast lights up on its turret old,
Yellow with moss and sea-fog mould.

Dreary the land when gust and sleet
At its doors and windows howl and beat,
And Winter laughs at its fires of peat!

But in summer time, when pool and pond,
Held in the laps of valleys fond,
Are blue as the glimpses of sea beyond;

When the hills are sweet with the brier-rose,
And, hid in the warm, soft dells, unclose
Flowers the mainland rarely knows;

When boats to their morning fishing go,
And, held to the wind and slanting low,
Whitening and darkening the small sails
      show,—

Then is that lonely island fair;
And the pale health-seeker findeth there
The wine of life in its pleasant air.

No greener valleys the sun invite,
On smoother beaches no sea-birds light,
No blue waves shatter to foam more white!

There, circling ever their narrow range,
Quaint tradition and legend strange
Live on unchallenged, and know no change.

Old wives spinning their webs of tow,
Or, rocking weirdly to and fro
In and out of the peat's dull glow,

And old men mending their nets of twine,
Talk together of dream and sign,
Talk of the lost ship Palatine,—

The ship that, a hundred years before,
Freighted deep with its goodly store,
In the gales of the equinox went ashore.

The eager islanders one by one
Counted the shots of her signal gun,
And heard the crash when she drove right
     on !

Into the teeth of death she sped :
(May God forgive the hands that fed
The false lights over the rocky Head !)

O men and brothers ! what sights were
     there !
White up-turned faces, hands stretched in
     prayer !
Where waves had pity, could ye not spare ?

Down swooped the wreckers, like birds of
     prey
Tearing the heart of the ship away,
And the dead had never a word to say.

And then, with ghastly shimmer and shine
Over the rocks and the seething brine,
They burned the wreck of the Palatine.

In their cruel hearts, as they homeward
        sped,
"The sea and the rocks are dumb," they
        said :
" There'll be no reckoning with the dead.'

But the year went round, and when once
        more
Along their foam-white curves of shore
They heard the line-storm rave and roar,

Behold ! again, with shimmer and shine,
Over the rocks and the seething brine,
The flaming wreck of the Palatine !

So, haply in fitter words than these,
Mending their nets on their patient knees
They tell the legend of Manisees.

Nor looks nor tones a doubt betray;
"It is known to us all," they quietly say;
"We too have seen it in our day."

Is there, then, no death for a word once
        spoken?
Was never a deed but left its token
Written on tables never broken?

Do the elements subtle reflections give?
Do pictures of all the ages live
On Nature's infinite negative,

Which, half in sport, in malice half,
She shows at times, with shudder or laugh,
Phantom and shadow in photograph?

For still, on many a moonless night,
From Kingston Head and from Montauk
        light
The spectre kindles and burns in sight.

Now low and dim, now clear and higher,
Leaps up the terrible Ghost of Fire,
Then, slowly sinking, the flames expire.

And the wise Sound skippers, though skies
        be fine,
Reef their sails when they see the sign
Of the blazing wreck of the Palatine !

———

  "A fitter tale to scream than sing,"
      The Book-man said.   "Well, fancy,
        then,"
  The Reader answered, "on the wing
      The sea-birds shriek it, not for men,

But in the ear of wave and breeze!"
The Traveller mused: "Your Manisees
Is fairy-land: off Narraganset shore
Who ever saw the isle or heard its name
    before?

"'Tis some strange land of Fly-away,
    Whose dreamy shore the ship beguiles,
St. Brandan's in its sea-mist gray,
    Or sunset loom of Fortunate Isles!"
"No ghost, but the solid turf and rock
Is the good island known as Block,"
The Reader said. "For beauty and for
    ease
I chose its Indian name, soft-flowing Mani-
    sees!

"But let it pass; here is a bit
    Of unrhymed story, with a hint

Of the old preaching mood in it,
    The sort of sidelong moral squint
Our friend objects to, which has grown,
I fear, a habit of my own.
'T was written when the Asian plague drew
        near,
And the land held its breath and paled with
        sudden fear."

ABRAHAM DAVENPORT.

In the old days (a custom laid aside
With breeches and cocked hats) the people
        sent
Their wisest men to make the public laws.
And so, from a brown homestead, where the
        Sound
Drinks the small tribute of the Mianas,
Waved over by the woods of Rippowams,

And hallowed by pure lives and tranquil
    deaths,
Stamford sent up to the councils of the State
Wisdom and grace in Abraham Davenport.

'T was on a May-day of the far old year
Seventeen hundred and eighty, that there
    fell
Over the bloom and sweet life of the Spring,
Over the fresh earth and the heaven of noon,
A horror of great darkness, like the night
In day of which the Norland sagas tell,—
The Twilight of the Gods.   The low-hung
    sky
Was black with ominous clouds, save where
    its rim
Was fringed with a dull glow, like that which
    climbs
The crater's sides from the red hell below.

Birds ceased to sing, and all the barn-yard
    fowls
Roosted ; the cattle at the pasture bars
Lowed, and looked homeward ; bats on
    leathern wings
Flitted abroad ; the sounds of labor died ;
Men prayed, and women wept ; all ears
    grew sharp
To hear the doom-blast of the trumpet
    shatter
The black sky, that the dreadful face of
    Christ
Might look from the rent clouds, not as he
    looked
A loving guest at Bethany, but stern
As Justice and inexorable Law.

Meanwhile in the old State-House, dim
    as ghosts,

Sat the lawgivers of Connecticut,

Trembling beneath their legislative robes.

" It is the Lord's Great Day !   Let us ad-
        journ,"

Some said ; and then, as if with one accord,

All eyes were turned to Abraham Daven-
        port.

He rose, slow cleaving with his steady voice

The intolerable hush.   " This well may be

The Day of Judgment which the world
        awaits ;

But be it so or not, I only know

My present duty, and my Lord's command

To occupy till he come.   So at the post

Where he hath set me in his providence,

I choose, for one, to meet him face to face,—

No faithful servant frightened from my task,

But ready when the Lord of the harvest
        calls ;

And therefore, with all reverence, I would
    say,
Let God do his work, we will see to ours.
Bring in the candles." And they brought
    them in.

  Then by the flaring lights the Speaker
    read,
Albeit with husky voice and shaking hands,
An act to amend, an act to regulate
The shad and alewive fisheries. Where-
    upon
Wisely and well spake Abraham Davenport,
Straight to the question, with no figures of
    speech
Save the ten Arab signs, yet not without
The shrewd dry humor natural to the man:
His awe-struck colleagues listening all the
    while,

Between the pauses of his argument,
To hear the thunder of the wrath of God
Break from the hollow trumpet of the cloud.

And there he stands in memory to this
        day,
Erect, self-poised, a rugged face, half seen
Against the background of unnatural dark,
A witness to the ages as they pass,
That simple duty hath no place for fear.

———

He ceased; just then the ocean seemed
    To lift a half-faced moon in sight;
And, shoreward, o'er the waters gleamed,
    From crest to crest, a line of light,
Such as of old, with solemn awe,
    The fishers by Gennesaret saw,
When dry-shod o'er it walked the Son of
        God,

Tracking the waves with light where'er his
    sandals trod.

  Silently for a space each eye
    Upon that sudden glory turned;
Cool from the land the breeze blew by,
    The tent-ropes flapped, the long beach
      churned
Its waves to foam; on either hand
Stretched, far as sight, the hills of sand;
With bays of marsh, and capes of bush and
    tree,
The wood's black shore-line loomed beyond
    the meadowy sea.

  The lady rose to leave.   "One song,
    Or hymn," they urged, "before we
      part."
And she, with lips to which belong
    Sweet intuitions of all art,

Gave to the winds of night a strain
　Which they who heard would bear again;
And to her voice the solemn ocean lent,
Touching its harp of sand, a deep accom-
　　paniment.

The harp at Nature's advent strung
　Has never ceased to play;
The song the stars of morning sung
　Has never died away.

And prayer is made, and praise is given,
　By all things near and far:
The ocean looketh up to heaven,
　And mirrors every star.

Its waves are kneeling on the strand,
　As kneels the human knee,
Their white locks bowing to the sand,
　The priesthood of the sea!

They pour their glittering treasures forth,
  Their gifts of pearl they bring,
And all the listening hills of earth
  Take up the song they sing.

The green earth sends her incense up
  From many a mountain shrine;
From folded leaf and dewy cup
  She pours her sacred wine.

The mists above the morning rills
  Rise white as wings of prayer;
The altar curtains of the hills
  Are sunset's purple air.

The winds with hymns of praise are loud,
  Or low with sobs of pain,—
The thunder-organ of the cloud,
  The dropping tears of rain.

With drooping head and branches crossed
　　The twilight forest grieves,
Or speaks with tongues of Pentecost
　　From all its sunlit leaves.

The blue sky is the temple's arch,
　　Its transept earth and air,
The music of its starry march
　　The chorus of a prayer.

So Nature keeps the reverent frame
　　With which her years began,
And all her signs and voices shame
　　The prayerless heart of man.

———

The singer ceased.　The moon's white rays
　　Fell on the rapt, still face of her.
" *Allah il Allah !*　He hath praise

From all things," said the Traveller.
" Oft from the desert's silent nights,
And mountain hymns of sunset lights,
My heart has felt rebuke, as in his tent
The Moslem's prayer has shamed by Chris-
    tian knee unbent."

He paused, and lo ! far, faint, and slow
    The bells in Newbury's steeples tolled
The twelve dead hours ; the lamp burned
        low ;
    The singer sought her canvas fold.
One sadly said, " At break of day
We strike our tent and go our way."
But one made answer cheerily, " Never fear,
We'll pitch this tent of ours in type another
        year."

THE PENNSYLVANIA PILGRIM.

PRELUDE.

I sing the Pilgrim of a softer clime
    And milder speech than those brave men's
        who brought
To the ice and iron of our winter time
    A will as firm, a creed as stern, and
        wrought
    With one mailed hand, and with the other
        fought.
Simply, as fits my theme, in homely rhyme
    I sing the blue-eyed German Spener
        taught.
Through whose veiled, mystic faith the
        Inward Light,
    Steady and still, an easy brightness, shone,
Transfiguring all things in its radiance white.

The garland which his meekness never
   sought
  I bring him ; over fields of harvest sown
  With seeds of blessing, now to ripeness
   grown,
I bid the sower pass before the reapers'
   sight.

THE
PENNSYLVANIA PILGRIM.

NEVER in tenderer quiet lapsed the day
From Pennsylvania's vales of spring away,
Where, forest-walled, the scattered hamlets
     lay

Along the wedded rivers.   One long bar
Of purple cloud, on which the evening star
Shone like a jewel on a scimitar,

Held the sky's golden gateway.   Through
     the deep
Hush of the woods a murmur seemed to
     creep,

The Schuylkill whispering in a voice of
    sleep.

All else was still. The oxen from their
    ploughs
Rested at last, and from their long day's
    browse
Came the dun files of Krisheim's home-
    bound cows.

And the young city, round whose virgin
    zone
The rivers like two mighty arms were thrown,
Marked by the smoke of evening fires
    alone,

Lay in the distance, lovely even then
With its fair women and its stately men
Gracing the forest court of William Penn,

Urban yet sylvan ; in its rough-hewn frames
Of oak and pine the dryads held their
    claims,
And lent its streets their pleasant woodland
    names.

Anna Pastorius down the leafy lane
Looked city-ward, then stooped to prune
    again
Her vines and simples, with a sigh of pain.

For fast the streaks of ruddy sunset paled
In the oak clearing, and, as daylight failed,
Slow, overhead, the dusky night-birds sailed.

Again she looked : between green walls of
    shade,
With low-bent head as if with sorrow
    weighed,
Daniel Pastorius slowly came and said,

"God's peace be with thee, Anna!" Then
      he stood
Silent before her, wrestling with the mood
Of one who sees the evil and not good.

" What is it, my Pastorius ? "   As she spoke,
A slow, faint smile across his features broke,
Sadder than tears.   " Dear heart," he said,
      " our folk

" Are even as others.   Yea, our goodliest
      Friends
Are frail ; our elders have their selfish ends,
And few dare trust the Lord to make amends

" For duty's loss.   So even our feeble word
For the dumb slaves the startled meeting
      heard
As if a stone its quiet waters stirred ;

"And, as the clerk ceased reading, there
　　began
A ripple of dissent which downward ran
In widening circles, as from man to man.

" Somewhat was said of running before sent,
Of tender fear that some their guide out-
　　went,
Troublers of Israel.　I was scarce intent

" On hearing, for behind the reverend row
Of gallery Friends, in dumb and piteous
　　show,
I saw, methought, dark faces full of woe,

" And in the spirit, I was taken where
They toiled and suffered ; I was made aware
Of shame and wrath and anguish and de-
　　spair !

" And while the meeting smothered our
     poor plea
With cautious phrase, a Voice there seemed
     to be,
' As ye have done to these ye do to me ! "

" So it all passed ; and the old tithe went on
Of anise, mint, and cumin, till the sun
Set, leaving still the weightier work undone.

" Help, for the good man faileth ! Who is
     strong,
If these be weak ? Who shall rebuke the
     wrong,
If these consent? How long, O Lord ! how
     long ! "

He ceased ; and, bound in spirit with the
     bound,

With folded arms, and eyes that sought the
    ground,
Walked musingly his little garden round.

About him, beaded with the falling dew,
Rare plants of power and herbs of healing
    grew,
Such as Van Helmont and Agrippa knew.

For, by the lore of Gorlitz' gentle sage,
With the mild mystics of his dreamy age
He read the herbal signs of nature's page,

At once he heard in sweet Von Merlau's
    bowers
Fair as herself, in boyhood's happy hours,
The pious Spener read his creed in flowers.

" The dear Lord give us patience ! " said his
    wife,

Touching with finger-tip an aloe, rife
With leaves sharp-pointed like an Aztec
    knife,

Or Carib spear, a gift to William Penn
From the rare gardens of John Evelyn,
Brought from the Spanish Main by mer-
    chantmen.

" See this strange plant this steady purpose
    hold,
And, year by year, its patient leaves unfold,
Till the young eyes that watched it first are
    old.

" But some time, thou hast told me, there
    shall come
A sudden beauty, brightness, and perfume,
The century-moulded bud shall burst in
    bloom.

" So may the seed which hath been sown
    to-day
Grow with the years, and, after long delay,
Break into bloom, and God's eternal Yea

" Answer at last the patient prayers of them
Who now, by faith alone, behold its stem
Crowned with the flowers of Freedom's
   diadem.

' Meanwhile, to feel and suffer, work and
    wait,
Remains for us.   The wrong indeed is great,
But love and patience conquer soon or late,"

" Well hast thou said, my Anna ! "   Ten-
    derer
Than youth's caress upon the head of her
Pastorius laid his hand.   " Shall we demur

" Because the vision tarrieth ?   In an hour
We dream not of the slow-grown bud may
    flower,
And what was sown in weakness rise in
    power ! "

Then through the vine-draped door whose
    legend read,
" Procul este profani ! " Anna led
To where their child upon his little bed

Looked up and smiled. " Deart heart," she
    said, " if we
Must bearers of a heavy burden be,
Our boy, God willing, yet the day shall see

" When, from the gallery to the farthest
    seat,
Slave and slave-owner shall no longer meet,
But all sit equal at the Master's feet."

On the stone hearth the blazing walnut
    block
Set the low walls a-glimmer, showed the cock
Rebuking Peter on the Van Wyck clock,

Shone on old tomes of law and physic, side
By side with Fox and Behmen, played at
    hide
And seek with Anna, midst her household
    pride

Of flaxen webs, and on the table, bare
Of costly cloth or silver cup, but where,
Tasting the fat shads of the Delaware,

The courtly Penn had praised the goodwife's
    cheer,
And quoted Horace o'er her home-brewed
    beer,
Till even grave Pastorius smiled to hear.

In such a home, beside the Schuylkill's wave,
He dwelt in peace with God and man, and
    gave
Food to the poor and shelter to the slave.

For all too soon the New World's scandal
    shamed
The righteous code by Penn and Sidney
    framed,
And men withheld the human rights they
    claimed.

And slowly wealth and station sanction lent,
And hardened avarice, on its gains intent,
Stifled the inward whisper of dissent.

Yet all the while the burden rested sore
On tender hearts. At last Pastorius bore
Their warning message to the Church's door

In God's name; and the leaven of the
    word
Wrought ever after in the souls who heard,
And a dead conscience in its grave-clothes
    stirred

To troubled life, and urged the vain excuse
Of Hebrew custom, patriarchal use,
Good in itself if evil in abuse.

Gravely Pastorius listened, not the less
Discerning through the decent fig-leaf dress
Of the poor plea its shame of selfishness.

One Scripture rule, at least, was unforgot;
He hid the outcast, and bewrayed him
    not;
And, when his prey the human hunter
    sought,

He scrupled not, while Anna's wise delay
And proffered cheer prolonged the master's
    stay,
To speed the black guest safely on his way.

Yet, who shall guess his bitter grief who
    lends
His life to some great cause, and finds his
    friends
Shame or betray it for their private ends?

How felt the Master when His chosen
    strove
In childish folly for their seats above;
And that fond mother, blinded by her love.

Besought Him that her sons, beside His
    throne,
Might sit on either hand? Amidst his own
A stranger oft, companionless and lone,

God's priest and prophet stands.   The
     martyr's pain
Is not alone from scourge and cell and chain ;
Sharper the pang when, shouting in his train,

His weak disciples by their lives deny
The loud hosannas of their daily cry,
And make their echo of His truth a lie.

His forest home no hermit's cell he found,
Guests, motley-minded, drew his hearth
     around,
And held armed truce upon its neutral
     ground.

There Indian chiefs with battle-bows un-
     strung,
Strong, hero-limbed, like those whom Ho-
     mer sung,
Pastorius fancied, when the world was young,

Came with their tawny women, lithe and tall,
Like bronzes in his friend Von Rodeck's
    hall,
Comely, if black, and not unpleasing all.

There hungry folk in homespun drab and
    gray
Drew round his board on Monthly Meeting
    day,
Genial, half merry in their friendly way.

Or, haply, pilgrims from the Fatherland,
Weak, timid, homesick, slow to understand
The New World's promise, sought his help-
    ing hand.

Or painful Kelpius from his hermit den
By Wissahickon, maddest of good men,
Dreamed o'er the Chiliast dreams of Peter-
    sen.

Deep in the woods, where the small river
    slid
Snake-like in shade, the Helmstadt Mystic
    hid,
Weird as a wizard over arts forbid,

Reading the books of Daniel and of John,
And Behmen's Morning-Redness, through
    the Stone
Of Wisdom, vouchsafed to his eyes alone,

Whereby he read what man ne'er read before,
And saw the visions man shall see no more,
Till the great angel, striding sea and shore,

Shall bid all flesh await, on land or ships,
The warning trump of the Apocalypse,
Shattering the heavens before the dread
    eclipse,

Or meek-eyed Mennonist his bearded chin
Leaned o'er the gate ; or Ranter, pure with-
            in,
Aired his perfection in a world of sin.

Or, talking of old home scenes, Op den
            Graaf
Teased the low back-log with his shodden
            staff,
Till the red embers broke into a laugh

And dance of flame, as if they fain would
            cheer
The rugged face, half tender, half austere,
Touched with the pathos of a homesick tear !

Or Sluyter, saintly familist, whose word
As law the Brethren of the Manor heard,
Announced the speedy terrors of the Lord,

And turned, like Lot at Sodom, from his
  race,
Above a wrecked world with complacent face
Riding secure upon his plank of grace !

Haply, from Finland's birchen groves exiled,
Manly in thought, in simple ways a child,
His white hair floating round his visage
  mild,

The Swedish pastor sought the Quaker's
  door,
Pleased from his neighbor's lips to hear once
  more
His long-disused and half-forgotten lore.

For both could baffle Babel's lingual curse,
And speak in Bion's Doric, and rehearse
Cleanthes' hymn or Virgil's sounding verse.

And oft Pastorius and the meek old man
Argued as Quaker and as Lutheran,
Ending in Christian love, as they began.

With lettered Lloyd on pleasant morns he
        strayed
Where Sommerhausen over vales of shade
Looked miles away, by every flower delayed,

Or song of bird, happy and free with one
Who loved, like him, to let his memory run
Over old fields of learning, and to sun

Himself in Plato's wise philosophies,
And dream with Philo over mysteries
Whereof the dreamer never finds the keys;

To touch all themes of thought, nor weakly
        stop

For doubt of truth, but let the buckets drop
Deep down and bring the hidden waters up.

For there was freedom in that wakening
   time
Of tender souls; to differ was not crime;
The varying bells made up the perfect chime.

On lips unlike was laid the altar's coal,
The white, clear light, tradition-colored,
   stole
Through the stained oriel of each human
   soul.

Gathered from many sects, the Quaker
   brought
His old beliefs, adjusting to the thought
That moved his soul the creed his fathers
   taught.

One faith alone, so broad that all mankind
Within themselves its secret witness find,
The soul's communion with the Eternal
    Mind,

The Spirit's law, the Inward Rule and Guide,
Scholar and peasant, lord and serf, allied,
The polished Penn and Cromwell's Iron-
    side.

As still in Hemskerck's Quaker Meeting,
    face
By face in Flemish detail, we may trace
How loose-mouthed boor and fine ancestral
    grace

Sat in close contrast,—the clipt-headed churl,
Broad market-dame, and simple serving-girl
By skirt of silk and periwig in curl!

For soul touched soul ; the spiritual treasure-
    trove
Made all men equal, none could rise above
Nor sink below that level of God's love.

So, with his rustic neighbors sitting down,
The homespun frock beside the scholar's
    gown,
Pastorius to the manners of the town

Added the freedom of the woods, and
    sought
The bookless wisdom by experience taught,
And learned to love his new-found home,
    while not

Forgetful of the old ; the seasons went
Their rounds, and somewhat to his spirit lent
Of their own calm and measureless content.

Glad even to tears, he heard the robin sing
His song of welcome to the Western spring,
And bluebird borrowing from the sky his
　　wing.

And when the miracle of autumn came,
And all the woods with many-colored flame
Of splendor, making summer's greenness
　　tame,

Burned, unconsumed, a voice without a sound
Spake to him from each kindled bush around,
And made the strange, new landscape holy
　　ground !

And when the bitter north-wind, keen and
　　swift,
Swept the white street and piled the door-
　　yard drift,
He exercised, as Friends might say, his gift

Of verse, Dutch, English, Latin, like the
    hash
Of corn and beans in Indian succotash;
Dull, doubtless, but with here and there a
    flash,

Of wit and fine conceit,—the good man's
    play
Of quiet fancies, meet to while away
The slow hours measuring off an idle day.

At evening, while his wife put on her look
Of love's endurance, from its niche he took
The written pages of his ponderous book,

And read, in half the languages of man,
His "Rusca Apium," which with bees
    began,
And through the gamut of creation ran.

Or, now and then, the missive of some
         friend
In gray Altorf or storied Nürnberg penned
Dropped in upon him like a guest to spend

The night beneath his roof-tree.   Mystical
The fair Von Merlau spake as waters fall
And voices sound in dreams, and yet withal

Human · and sweet, as if each far, low
         tone,
Over the roses of her gardens blown,
Brought the warm sense of beauty all her
         own.

Wise Spener questioned what his friend
         could trace
Of spiritual influx or of saving grace
In the wild natures of the Indian race.

And learned Schurmberg, fain, at times, to
    look
From Talmud, Koran, Veds, and Pentateuch,
Sought out his pupil in his far-off nook,

To query with him of climatic change,
Of bird, beast, reptile, in his forest range,
Of flowers and fruits and simples new and
    strange.

And thus the Old and New World reached
    their hands
Across the water, and the friendly lands
Talked with each other from their severed
    strands.

Pastorius answered all: while seed and root
Sent from his new home grew to flower and
    fruit
Along the Rhine and at the Spessart's foot;

And, in return, the flowers his boyhood
　　knew
Smiled at his door, the same in form and
　　hue,
And on his vines the Rhenish clusters grew.

No idler he ; whoever else might shirk,
He set his hand to every honest work,—
Farmer and teacher, court and meeting clerk.

Still on the town seal his device is found,
Grapes, flax, and thread-spool on a trefoil
　　ground,
With "VINUM, LINUM ET TEXTRINUM"
　　wound.

One house sufficed for gospel and for law,
Where Paul and Grotius, Scripture text and
　　saw,
Assured the good, and held the rest in awe.

Whatever legal maze he wandered through,
He kept the Sermon on the Mount in view.
And justice always into mercy grew.

No whipping-post he needed, stocks, nor jail,
Nor ducking-stool; the orchard-thief grew
       pale
At his rebuke, the vixen ceased to rail,

The usurer's grasp released the forfeit land;
The slanderer faltered at the witness-stand,
And all men took his counsel for command.

Was it caressing air, the brooding love
Of tenderer skies than German land knew of,
Green calm below, blue quietness above,

Still flow of water, deep repose of wood
That, with a sense of loving Fatherhood
And childlike trust in the Eternal Good,

Softened all hearts, and dulled the edge of
    hate,
Hushed strife, and taught impatient zeal to
    wait
The slow assurance of the better state?

Who knows what goadings in their sterner
    way
O'er jagged ice, relieved by granite gray,
Blew round the men of Massachusetts Bay?

What hate of heresy the east-wind woke?
What hints of pitiless power and terror
    spoke
In waves that on their iron coast-line broke?

Be it as it may : within the Land of Penn
The sectary yielded to the citizen,
And peaceful dwelt the many-creeded men.

Peace brooded over all.   No trumpet stung
The air to madness, and no steeple flung
Alarums down from bells at midnight rung.

The land slept well.   The Indian from his
    face
Washed all his war-paint off, and in the
    place
Of battle-marches sped the peaceful chase,

Or wrought for wages at the white man's
    side,—
Giving to kindness what his native pride
And lazy freedom to all else denied.

And well the curious scholar loved the old
Traditions that his swarthy neighbors told
By wigwam-fires when nights were growing
    cold,

Discerned the fact round which their fancy
    drew
Its dreams, and held their childish faith
    more true
To God and man than half the creeds he
    knew.

The desert blossomed round him ; wheat-
    fields rolled
Beneath the warm wind waves of green and
    gold ;
The planted ear returned its hundred-fold.

Great clusters ripened in a warmer sun
Than that which by the Rhine stream shines
    upon
The purpling hillsides with low vines o'er-
    run.

About each rustic porch the humming-bird

Tried with light bill, that scarce a petal
    stirred,
The Old World flowers to virgin soil trans-
    ferred ;

And the first-fruits of pear and apple, bend-
    ing
The young boughs down, their gold and
    russet blending,
Made glad his heart, familiar odors lending

To the fresh fragrance of the birch and pine,
Life-everlasting, bay, and eglantine,
And all the subtle scents the woods com-
    bine.

Fair First-Day mornings, steeped in sum-
    mer calm
Warm, tender, restful, sweet with woodland
    balm,

Came to him, like some mother-hallowed
    psalm

To the tired grinder at the noisy wheel
Of labor, winding off from memory's reel
A golden thread of music.   With no peal

Of bells to call them to the house of praise,
The scattered settlers through green forest-
    ways
Walked meeting-ward.   In reverent amaze

The Indian trapper saw them, from the dim
Shade of the alders on the rivulet's rim,
Seek the Great Spirit's house to talk with
    Him.

There, through the gathered stillness mul-
    tiplied

And made intense by sympathy, outside
The sparrows sang, and the gold-robin
    cried,

A-swing upon his elm.   A faint perfume
Breathed through the open windows of the
    room
From locust-trees, heavy with clustered
    bloom.

Thither, perchance, sore-tried confessors
    came,
Whose fervor jail nor pillory could tame,
Proud of the cropped ears meant to be their
    shame,

Men who had eaten slavery's bitter bread
In Indian isles; pale women who had bled
Under the hangman's lash, and bravely said

God's message through their prison's iron
        bars ;
And gray old soldier-converts, seamed with
        scars
From every stricken field of England's wars.

Lowly before the Unseen Presence knelt
Each waiting heart, till haply some one felt
On his moved lips the seal of silence melt.

Or, without spoken words, low breathings
        stole
Of a diviner life from soul to soul,
Baptizing in one tender thought the whole.

When shaken hands announced the meeting
        o'er,
The friendly group still lingered at the
        door,
Greeting, inquiring, sharing all the store

Of weekly tidings. Meanwhile youth and
    maid
Down the green vistas of the woodland
    strayed,
Whispered and smiled and oft their feet
    delayed.

Did the boy's whistle answer back the
    thrushes?
Did light girl laughter ripple through the
    bushes,
As brooks make merry over roots and rushes?

Unvexed the sweet air seemed. Without a
    wound
The ear of silence heard, and every sound
Its place in nature's fine accordance found.

And solemn meeting, summer sky and
    wood,

Old kindly faces, youth and maidenhood
Seemed, like God's new creation, very good!

And, greeting all with quiet smile and word,
Pastorius went his way.   The unscared bird
Sang at his side ; scarcely the squirrel stirred

At his hushed footstep on the mossy sod ;
And, wheresoe'er the good man looked or
        trod,
He felt the peace of nature and of God.

His social life wore no ascetic form,
He loved all beauty, without fear of harm,
And in his veins his Teuton blood ran
        warm.

Strict to himself, of other men no spy,
He made his own no circuit-judge to try
The freer conscience of his neighbors by.

With love rebuking, by his life alone,
Gracious and sweet, the better way was
     shown,
The joy of one, who, seeking not his own,

And faithful to all scruples, finds at last
The thorns and shards of duty overpast,
And daily life, beyond his hope's forecast,

Pleasant and beautiful with sight and sound,
And flowers upspringing in its narrow round,
And all his days with quiet gladness crowned.

He sang not; but, if sometimes tempted
     strong,
He hummed what seemed like Altorf's
     Burschensong,
His goodwife smiled, and did not count it
     wrong.

For well he loved his boyhood's brother
    band ;
His Memory, while he trod the New
    World's strand,
A double-ganger walked the Fatherland !

If, when on frosty Christmas eves the
    light
Shone on his quiet hearth, he missed the
    sight
Of Yule-log, Tree, and Christ-child all in
    white ;

And closed his eyes, and listened to the
    sweet
Old wait-songs sounding down his native
    street,
And watched again the dancers' mingling
    feet ;

Yet not the less, when once the vision
    passed,
He held the plain and sober maxims fast
Of the dear Friends with whom his lot was
    cast.

Still all attuned to nature's melodies,
He loved the bird's song in his dooryard
    trees,
And the low hum of home-returning bees ;

The blossomed flax, the tulip-trees in bloom
Down the long street, the beauty and per-
    fume
Of apple-boughs, the mingling light and
    gloom

Of Sommerhausen's woodlands, woven
    through

With sun-threads ; and the music the wind
     drew,
Mournful and sweet, from leaves it over-
     blew.

And evermore, beneath this outward sense,
And through the common sequence of
     events,
He felt the guiding hand of Providence

Reach out of space.   A Voice spake in his ear,
And lo ! all other voices far and near
Died at that whisper, full of meanings clear.

The Light of Life shone round him ; one
     by one
The wandering lights, that all-misleading
     run,
Went out like candles paling in the sun.

That Light he followed, step by step, where'er
It led, as in the vision of the seer
The wheels moved as the spirit in the clear

And terrible crystal moved, with all their eyes
Watching the living splendor sink or rise,
Its will their will, knowing no otherwise.

Within himself he found the law of right,
He walked by faith and not the letter's sight,
And read his Bible by the Inward Light.

And if sometimes the slaves of form and rule,
Frozen in their creeds like fish in winter's pool,
Tried the large tolerance of his liberal school,

His door was free to men of every name,
He welcomed all the seeking souls who
    came,
And no man's faith he made a cause of
    blame.

But best he loved in leisure hours to see
His own dear Friends sit by him knee to
    knee,
In social converse, genial, frank, and free.

There sometimes silence (it were hard to
    tell
Who owned it first) upon the circle fell,
Hushed Anna's busy wheel, and laid its
    spell

On the black boy who grimaced by the
    hearth,

To solemnize his shining face of mirth ;
Only the old clock ticked amidst the dearth

Of sound ; nor eye was raised nor hand was
     stirred
In that soul-sabbath, till at last some word
Of tender counsel or low prayer was heard.

Then guests, who lingered but farewell to say
And take love's message, went their home-
     ward way ;
So passed in peace the guileless Quaker's day.

His was the Christian's unsung Age of Gold,
A truer idyl than the bards have told
Of Arno's banks or Arcady of old.

Where still the Friends their place of burial
     keep,

And century-rooted mosses o'er it creep.
The Nürnberg scholar and his helpmeet
    sleep.

And Anna's aloe?   If it flowered at last
In Bartram's garden, did John Woolman cast
A glance upon it as he meekly passed?

And did a secret sympathy possess
That tender soul, and for the slave's redress
Lend hope, strength, patience?   It were
    vain to guess.

Nay, were the plant itself but mythical,
Set in the fresco of tradition's wall
Like Jotham's bramble, mattereth not at all.

Enough to know that, through the winter's
    frost

And summer's heat, no seed of truth is lost,
And every duty pays at last its cost.

For, ere Pastorius left the sun and air,
God sent the answer to his lifelong prayer;
The child was born beside the Delaware,

Who, in the power a holy purpose lends,
Guided his people unto nobler ends,
And left them worthier of the name of
      Friends.

And lo! the fulness of the time has come,
And over all the exile's Western home,
From sea to sea the flowers of freedom
      bloom!

And joy-bells ring, and silver trumpets blow;
But not for thee, Pastorius!   Even so
The world forgets, but the wise angels know.

THE MANTLE OF SAINT JOHN DE MATHA.

A LEGEND OF "THE RED, WHITE AND BLUE,"
A. D. 1154–1864.

A STRONG and mighty Angel,
　Calm, terrible, and bright,
The cross in blended red and blue
　Upon his mantle white !

Two captives by him kneeling,
　Each on his broken chain,
Sang praise to God who raiseth
　The dead to life again !

Dropping his cross-wrought mantle,
  "Wear this," the Angel said;
"Take thou, O Freedom's priest, its sign,—
  The white, the blue, and red."

Then rose up John De Matha
  In the strength the Lord Christ gave,
And begged through all the land of France
  The ransom of the slave.

The gates of tower and castle
  Before him open flew,
The drawbridge at his coming fell,
  The door-bolt backward drew.

For all men owned his errand,
  And paid his righteous tax;
And the hearts of lord and peasant
  Were in his hands as wax

At last, outbound from Tunis,
  His bark her anchor weighed,
Freighted with seven score Christian souls
  Whose ransom he had paid.

But, torn by Paynim hatred,
  Her sails in tatters hung;
And on the wild waves, rudderless
  A shattered hulk she swung.

"God save us!" cried the captain,
  "For naught can man avail:
O, woe betide the ship that lacks
  Her rudder and her sail!

"Behind us are the Moormen;
  At sea we sink or strand:
There's death upon the water,
  There's death upon the land!"

Then up spake John De Matha:
  " God's errands never fail!
Take thou the mantle which I wear,
  And make of it a sail."

They raised the cross-wrought mantle,
  The blue, the white, the red ;
And straight before the wind off-shore
  The ship of Freedom sped.

" God help us ! " cried the seamen,
  " For vain is mortal skill :
The good ship on a stormy sea
  Is drifting at its will."

Then up spake John De Matha :
  " My mariners, never fear !
The Lord whose breath has filled her sail
  May well our vessel steer ! "

So on through storm and darkness
　　They drove for weary hours ;
And lo ! the third gray morning shone
　　On Ostia's friendly towers.

And on the walls the watchers
　　The ship of mercy knew,—
They knew far off its holy cross,
　　The red, the white, and blue.

And the bells in all the steeples
　　Rang out in glad accord,
To welcome home to Christian soil
　　The ransomed of the Lord.

So runs the ancient legend
　　By bard and painter told ;
And lo ! the cycle rounds again,
　　The new is as the old !

With rudder foully broken,
  And sails by traitors torn,
Our country on a midnight sea
  Is waiting for the morn.

Before her, nameless terror ;
  Behind, the pirate foe ;
The clouds are black above her,
  The sea is white below.

The hope of all who suffer,
  The dread of all who wrong,
She drifts in darkness and in storm,
  How long, O Lord, how long ?

But courage, O my mariners !
  Ye shall not suffer wreck,
While up to God the freedman's prayers
  Are rising from your deck.

Is not your sail the banner
  Which God hath blest anew,
The mantle that De Matha wore,
  The red, the white, the blue?

Its hues are all of heaven,—
  The red of sunset's dye,
The whiteness of the moon-lit cloud,
  The blue of morning's sky.

Wait cheerily then, O mariners,
  For daylight and for land;
The breath of God is in your sail,
  Your rudder is His hand.

Sail on, sail on, deep-freighted
  With blessings and with hopes;
The saints of old with shadowy hands
  Are pulling at your ropes.

Behind ye holy martyrs
   Uplift the palm and crown ;
Before ye unborn ages send
   Their benedictions down.

Take heart from John De Matha !—
   God's errands never fail !
Sweep on through storm and darkness,
   The thunder and the hail !

Sail on !   The morning cometh,
   The port ye yet shall win ;
And all the bells of God shall ring
   The good ship bravely in !